Museum Villages - USA

NICHOLAS ZOOK

Museum Villages
USA

BARRE PUBLISHERS • 1971
Barre, Massachusetts

The Deserted Village at Allaire, New Jersey, is a restored period piece

For Audrey, my wife,
to whom I owe so much

Contents

1. The American Heritage   7

2. Indian Villages   15

3. First Settlements and Colonial Towns   29

4. Life in the New Republic   42

5. The Westward Migration   58

6. The Gold and Silver Rush   69

7. Lincoln and the Civil War   80

8. The Wild West   88

9. That Old-Time Religion   94

10. Iron, Lumber and Farm Villages   109

11. A Word on Walking Tours   117

12. A Directory of Museum Villages   126

Photo Credits   136

The Geddy House and silversmith shop at Colonial Williamsburg

1

The American Heritage

AMERICANS today are more conscious of their country's history, more aware of their own unique heritage, than ever before. This is nowhere more apparent than in the field of restoration, reconstruction and preservation, a field which has touched in some measure virtually every large community in the Republic.

In no other country have such vast sums of money been expended for the rescue and refurbishing of old and significant sites and structures. In no other country have so many dedicated individuals donated so much time and energy to preserve historic landmarks in order that this generation, and future generations, might share through them the trials and glory of our forebears.

Here, across the entire length and width of our land, are factories, shops, bridges, mine shafts, homes, entire communities built with hope and high purpose by earlier Americans. These are not decaying structures, destined in time for oblivion. These are carefully tended monuments, zealously guarded by government agencies, associations and individuals and intended to reflect truly an earlier manner of life.

Many are national historic sites. The American flag is proudly raised each dawn at Appomattox Court House National Park in Virginia, site of the surrender of Confederate forces to General Ulysses S. Grant by General Robert E. Lee on Palm Sunday, April 9, 1865. The Herbert Hoover Birthplace, along with adjacent town streets, has been restored in West Branch, Iowa. The charcoal-burning cold-blast furnace which provided needed iron during the Revolutionary War is a part of the Hopewell Village National Historic Site in Pennsylvania.

Others are the property of historical groups. Old Hickory's Hermitage in Nashville, Tennessee, comprised of a number of outstanding buildings associated with Andrew Jackson, is maintained by the Ladies Hermitage Association. A Pioneer Farm Museum and Western Reserve Village in Bath, Ohio, is owned and administered by the Western Reserve Historical Society. The stone house community built in New Paltz, New York, by the French Huguenots in the 17th century is the property of the Huguenot Historic Society.

Still others are the hobby of those who seek only to recreate through buildings and antique objects a small segment of other centuries. Shelburne Museum in Vermont, with its vast collection of Americana in 35 buildings, was the outgrowth of an antiques collection amassed through years by its founder, Mrs. Electra Havemeyer Webb. The Old Museum Village of Smith's Clove in Monroe, New York, evolved through the dedication of

Roscoe W. Smith to his extensive collection of tools that built America. Calico Ghost Town, once Southern California's greatest silver camp, was bought and restored through the efforts of Walter Knott, member of a pioneer family and a prominent businessman.

To deal with all phases of the preservation movement would be a monumental task. The purpose of this volume is to concentrate on those building complexes which fall into the category of "museum villages." Its secondary aim is to pay tribute to and to spotlight significant communities which offer a broad glimpse of yesteryear through walking tours or open-house pilgrimages.

The museum villages of the United States—and there are more than a hundred of them—are a far-flung tapestry of American history, splendid in detail and capable of projecting you into time past. Here, in its infinite variety, is the breadth of life as our forebears—the pioneers, the miners, the gunmen of the Old West, the fishermen who went to sea—knew it.

The villages are tellers of tales. They will speak to you—through homes, portraits and docu-ments—of love and hate, of peace and war, of life and death. Theirs are the stories of hundreds of thousands of men, women and children who once shared, as you do now, a knowledge and a dependence on this land. Some of the stories are not pretty ones. Artifacts, letters and manuscripts in some of the villages bear testament to the ferocity of Indian massacres and slow death by starvation. Ghost towns and "boot hill" cemeteries will hint at lost dreams, avarice and lawlessness. But all the tales are of people who inhabited this land, including those who were a part of civilizations long gone.

High above the semi-arid plains in the southwest corner of Colorado, Pueblo Indians built large communities of cliff dwellings in massive recesses below the canyon cliffs of Mesa Verde. For about 80 years from 1200 A.D., they shaped stone blocks with stone axes for structures with as many as two hundred rooms. Mud served as their mortar and packed clay as their flooring. The dwellings housed not only living quarters but ceremonial and religious chambers. The tribe vanished from the site about 1300 A.D., leaving its

Pueblo of Kuana in Coronado State Monument, New Mexico

8

Old hotel stands as memorial to Gold Rush days near Gilmore, Idaho

more than 500 cliff dwellings to decay in solitude for nearly six centuries. Today, you may visit this ancient village in its carefully preserved state within the Mesa Verde National Park.

The stories trace the American experience from the first coast settlements by the white man in the 16th century through and beyond the age of the Industrial Revolution in the 19th century. These stories will bring you close to early American legends and to comparatively recent American folk lore.

The struggles of the first permanent English settlers in America are dramatized in Virginia's Jamestown Festival Park where James Fort has been reconstructed, duplicating the simple homes of the first 105 settlers in Virginia in 1607. This was the primitive settlement that made legendary heroes of Captain John Smith, John Rolfe and Pocahontas. The weakened and starving colonists constantly faced a more sudden death at the hands of hostile Indians when Captain Smith went foraging for food. He was captured by Indians and led, apparently for execution, before their great chief Powhatan. As hope for survival dimmed,

"Pocahontas the Kings dearest daughter, when no intreaty could prevaile, got his head in her armes, and laid her owne upon his to save him from death."

Strawbery Banke in Portsmouth, New Hampshire, reflects the initial tide of prosperity that created great mansions in a major port of colonial America. In this authentic restoration of an early seaport town the original homes of sea captains, shipbuilders and artisans appear as they did in the 17th, 18th and 19th centuries.

You will learn in a great number of museum villages that religious persecution forced hundreds of thousands of persons to flee Europe. It was in America that refugees sought to form their own utopias, many of them embracing new concepts of communal life. From Germany, England, France and Sweden they came, building churches in the wilderness and turning forest into farmland. Sturdy villages today are a testament to the determination and industry of such sects as the Huguenots, Shakers, Harmonists and Moravians.

With a new freedom gained by the Revolutionary War, Americans inevitably turned to the

Sherburne House at Strawbery Banke, New Hampshire, dates from 1695

Pioneer life is reflected in Hale Farm Museum, Bath, Ohio

unexplored and legendary West, seeking a better life and possible fortune. Steadily the huge land areas that knew only the cry of the Indian were dotted with the sprouting settlements of the white man. Many New Englanders poured into the Western Reserve territory of Ohio. A reconstructed village in Bath stands as a memorial to the pioneers and the manner in which they cleared the land, built log cabins and later replaced them with more substantial homes.

Lumbermen by the thousands swarmed in the 19th century into Wisconsin, Michigan and northern Illinois during a lumber boom which lasted nearly a century. Millions of acres of fine timberland were the magnet which drew them, and many of the camps they established are today prosperous communities. The story of the rough and ready lumberjack is told in the Paul Bunyan camp in Eau Claire, Wisconsin. This logging camp with its tools, sleighs and bunkhouses immortalizes a pioneering enterprise that vanished when the region was stripped of its tall white pine.

The Wild West and the law of the six-gun is epitomized in towns like Tombstone, Arizona, a boom town born of a rich silver strike. Its early days, when Wyatt Earp was sheriff, are re-enacted every year. Some of its buildings house possessions of the Earps, Doc Holliday and Bat Masterson. Its nearby Boot Hill Cemetery is the resting place of many gunmen who were not too tough to die.

You may glimpse the era of the covered wagon at Fort Laramie, a national historic site in Wyoming. The fort began as a fur-trading center in 1834 and progressed to become the main Army post west of the Mississippi from 1849 to 1890. It grew into a fortified village of 86 structures, serving waves of pioneer emigrants headed for Oregon and California. Covered wagon caravans stopped here to repair their outfits and to give their animals a rest. The Mormons, driven out of Missouri and Illinois and seeking more peaceful pastures, used Fort Laramie as a way station.

These are a fraction of the stories that the village museums have to tell. And, by their very existence, they will tell you of individuals and groups who through the decades have championed the cause of historic preservation. The champions were

comparatively few in the 19th century when newly discovered ruins of Indian cliff dwellings and pueblos were being vandalized in the Southwest. The extent of the vandalism was such that the New England Historic Genealogical Society petitioned Congress, through Senator George F. Hoar of Massachusetts, to protect the archaeological sites. It was seven years before Congress appropriated $2000 for the protection of the Casa Grande ruins in Arizona. It was another three years before President Harrison, on June 22, 1892, issued an executive order reserving the site of the homes built by Indians who had farmed the Gila Valley more than 600 years before. In 1918 the area was placed under the administration of the National Park Service and designated a National Monument.

With this precedent, the gradual acquisition by the federal government of other historic sites was inevitable. It included, in 1906, the establishment of the Mesa Verde National Park of Colorado, with its notable cliff dwellings on view in its 50,000 acres. It has since included Presidents' homes, battlefields, forts and the sites of early industry.

The role of the individual in the cause of preservation has long been a major one. An example is William Randolph Hearst, the newspaper publisher, who bought the deserted village of New Salem, Illinois, in 1906. It was in this village that Abraham Lincoln arrived in 1831 as a youth without purpose and left it six years later as a lawyer and member of the General Assembly. The village has been recreated and is today a state park. This is the community as Lincoln knew it as he clerked in a store, chopped wood, served as postmaster and failed in a retail business.

No individual gave as freely of his time and money as John D. Rockefeller Jr. in his restoration—among others—of Colonial Williamsburg in Virginia. This was a project which set a fine example of what could be done by way of restoring a historic community as a whole. The project was first the dream of the late Reverend William A. R. Goodwin, rector of Bruton Parish Church in Williamsburg, a dream conceived in the early 1920s of restoring a large portion of the town which had been the capital of Virginia from 1699 to 1780. Dr. Goodwin expressed his hope and

Cliff dwellings,
circa 1000–1300 A.D.,
Manitou Springs, Colorado

13

outlined a plan for preservation to Rockefeller during the latter's visit to Williamsburg in 1926. In the following year Rockefeller decided to support the "endeavor to restore accurately and to preserve for all time the most significant portions of an historic and important city of America's colonial period."

The project was a gigantic one. Some 600 buildings, erected in the 19th and 20th centuries, were torn down or moved outside the restoration area. Singly and in groups, buildings were restored or rebuilt and opened to the public, beginning in 1932. Today, the 130-acre historic area includes more than eighty original 18th century structures and ninety gardens.

During the years of this century the role of groups and organizations has been ever greater. One of the first organizations formed for the sole purpose of historic preservation was the Society for the Preservation of New England Antiquities, founded in 1910 to "preserve for future generations the rapidly disappearing architectural monuments of New England and the smaller antiquities connected with its people." Similar organizations sprang up throughout the country, rescuing a historic or architecturally unique building here and an entire village there.

The awareness for the need of preservation became so keen that some groups appeared to form spontaneously, as they did not too long ago in the Berkshire hills of Massachusetts. It was in the town of Hancock that three remaining members of the United Society of Believers in Christ's Second Appearing, known more commonly as the Shakers, closed their community in 1960. Here was one of 19 Shaker communities established in this country, a community which at its height had a total membership of about 300 believers. Public-spirited citizens in the Berkshires formed Shaker Community, Inc., and bought the property. The organization has restored 12 of 18 buildings on the 935-acre site and furnished them authentically.

It is through such efforts that the number of museum villages continues to increase. It is because of such dedication that history, culture and the breath of life past await your appraisal in America's museum villages.

Berry-Lincoln Store is preserved at New Salem State Park, Illinois

2

Indian Villages

THE LAND of the Americas was Indian land for thousands of years before the Spanish, Portuguese, French, English and others planted their individual flags on the two continents and claimed possession of portions of them.

Scientists believe the first human beings came to America by way of a land bridge between Siberia and Alaska, perhaps 10,000 to 15,000 years ago. It is probable that the migrants came in successive waves. Certainly they multiplied, splintering into units which spread throughout South and North America. Through the centuries the migrants evolved into tribes with their own characteristics, culture and language. Most of the hundreds of tribes which flourished before the advent of the white man have long vanished.

Throughout the United States today, the Indian past is evident in place names, artifacts and earthworks. Museums in many states tell small portions of the Indian story. But nowhere is the Indian way of life more dramatically portrayed than in the comparatively few museum villages.

Many prehistoric village ruins tell volumes about the golden age of the Indians of the Southwest, the Hohokam, the Anasazi, the Pueblo, who predated by centuries the arrival of the white man. That age was witness to a culture in which arts and crafts, advanced agriculture and remarkable building techniques flourished.

Typical of this culture was that of the peaceful Hohokam tribe, which roughly 2000 years ago settled the plain stretching through much of Arizona into Mexico. It was an agricultural tribe, growing corn, then unknown to the Western world, along with cotton, beans and squash. It made the hot plain fertile by channeling water through miles of irrigation ditches from the Gila River to the north. By 1000 A.D. the irrigation system in the Gila Valley was a crisscross pattern made up of more than 200 miles of shallow canals. At first the Hohokam lived in small, scattered villages of single-room houses built of mud and brush. But about 1150 A.D. a group of Pueblo farmers migrated into the area, bringing with them new ideas for home building. Thus began an era when large communal houses of stone or clay were erected.

The Casa Grande Ruins, a national monument in Arizona, has six prehistoric villages, including massive cliff dwellings, within its boundaries, tracing the cultural progress of the Hohokam.

Among these is the Casa Grande, or Big House, a unique four-story structure of coursed caliche-earth construction, built about 600 years ago to

15

serve as apartment house, fortress and ceremonial building for its occupants.

Rich in prehistoric ruins, Arizona has other remarkable cliff houses and pueblos built by the Pueblo Indians, at Tuzigoot National Monument near Clarkdale and at Canyon de Chelly National Monument northwest of Gallup. At Tuzigoot, a gigantic pueblo covered the summit of a cliff that rises 120 feet above the Verde Valley. In places, the pueblo was two stories high, with its 77 ground-floor rooms covering an area about 500 feet long and 100 feet wide. At Canyon de Chelly, the communal dwellings were nestled below towering cliffs or perched on high ledges.

Perhaps the most impressive monument to the civilization of the Pueblo Indians is located in Colorado's

MESA VERDE NATIONAL PARK

The Pueblo Indians were descendants of the Anasazi tribes that settled in the Southwest some 2000 years ago. Their skill at farming, basket-making and other crafts increased through the centuries. Their village evolved from clusters of circular pit houses, their earth floors below ground level, to above-ground structures of adobe.

Later, clans pooled their resources and labor to build homes of contiguous rooms. The outside walls of a structure were extended to add two or three rooms at a time. In addition to living quarters, the clans added storage rooms and ceremonial chambers, or kivas, from which women were barred.

By 1100 A.D. this concept of apartment-house living had spread throughout the plain region. For the next 200 years building techniques improved, until the tribes vanished from the region, probably the aftermath of a long drought. Communal buildings were erected from precisely measured stone blocks on tops of mesas, creating pueblos, and in the recesses of cliff walls to form cliff dwellings.

In Mesa Verde, on a majestic plateau rising abruptly out of semi-arid land, you may see the manner in which building methods evolved from 600 to 1276 A.D. The early pit houses are crude indeed when compared with the Cliff Palace, built into a cave about 300 feet long and 100 feet deep. This ancient apartment house, from one to four stories in height, has more than 200 rooms, some with fireplaces and walls decorated with paintings.

Also in Colorado are the Manitou Cliff Dwellings, near Manitou Springs. Here, beneath overhanging cliffs, are the homes and artifacts of various Southwestern cliff dwellers. Unlike Mesa Verde, these dwellings are not on their original locations but were removed from various unprotected sites and reconstructed in detail as part of an outdoor museum.

Other villages of prehistoric Indians are maintained in New Mexico as national monuments:

GILA CLIFF DWELLINGS

The Gila Cliff Dwellings, north of Silver City, New Mexico, lie at the edge of the Gila National Forest, the nation's first designated wilderness area, in surroundings much as they were when the cliff dwellings were built. Earliest ruins within the preserve are remains of pit houses built by the Mogollon tribe in the centuries after 100 A.D., but again the focus is on the more refined structures which were patterned a thousand years later after the Pueblo apartment houses.

A self-guiding trail at Gila will take you past natural caves in the face of a cliff, containing the ruins of dwellings which housed many families. It will also take you along well-preserved apartment houses with T-shaped windows, ventilation holes and precisely measured beams which served as roof supports. Here are such refinements as stone cavities which were storage bins and stone benches which served as beds.

CHACO CANYON

Chaco Canyon National Monument, 96 miles from Gallup, New Mexico, was the Pueblo Indian's center of trade. The major section of the monument contains a dozen great ruins and more than 300 archaeological sites in an area about two miles wide and eight miles long.

Greatest of the pueblos here is Pueblo Bonito, an apartment dwelling with about 800 rooms capable of housing 1200 persons. The pueblo, which covered three acres, had 32 kivas. Excavation at the site of the kivas has uncovered fine ceremonial objects, such as ornaments of jet and shell and necklaces of turquoise beads.

AZTEC RUINS

The Aztec Ruins National Monument, 14 miles east of Farmington, New Mexico, has within its 27 acres the ruins of one of the largest pre-Spanish villages in the Southwest. The ruin, once a three-

Casa Grande Ruins,
protected by large roof

17

Pueblo Bonito at Chaco Canyon is ruin of large apartment house

*Casa Rinconada, largest excavated great kiva
in New Mexico, located at Chaco Canyon*

story building of 500 rooms, is regarded as an excellent example of classical pueblo construction. Tree-ring dates indicate that most of the gigantic structure was built from 1110 to 1114. Erected around a rectangular plaza, it consisted mainly of one-story housing units with rear units terraced up to three stories. Rooms were about 10 by 12 feet, with ceilings nine feet high.

An archaeological excavation of a different kind has shed new light on a tribe of Indians that flourished in Tennessee before the first white colonists established a foothold.

CHUCALISSA INDIAN VILLAGE

Eight miles from Memphis, Tennessee, Chucalissa Indian Town is an archaeological development and museum directed by Memphis State University. The village is partly staffed by Choctaw Indians, who act as guides and work on the site at native crafts.

This was a thriving Indian settlement from 900 to about 1600 A.D., when its inhabitants for some reason abandoned it. At its peak it had more than 1000 residents who lived in thatched-roof houses, farmed the land and built great earthworks.

The site was called to the attention of archaeologists by Civilian Conservations Corps workers in the late 1930s and was visited by a field party from the University of Tennessee in 1940. Amateur scientists in the area, who excavated portions of the site as a hobby, succeeded in having the village established as a state park in 1955.

Since 1962 Chucalissa has been operated as a research, student training and public education center by Memphis State University. The university gave the village its name of Chucalissa, meaning "house abandoned or deserted town." It has reconstructed 10 native houses and furnished several of them with authentic artifacts. Of particular interest is a 60-foot diameter temple, built atop a pyramidal mound where a high priest once tended the sacred fire. On the macabre side is an excavated area which has been roofed over. Here the remains of 40 persons show burial customs practiced during the early and later stages of the village's occupancy.

OCONALUFTEE INDIAN VILLAGE

The historian John Lawson listed 29 Indian tribes in writing about North Carolina in 1709. These included the Croatans, who inhabited Roanoke Island, and the Cherokee, who made the northern Allegheny Mountains their home.

Ceremonial chamber at Aztec National Monument, New Mexico

Burial practices on view at Chucalissa Indian Village

A mountain people, the Cherokee placed more emphasis on hunting than on agriculture. The tribe occupied portions of North Carolina, Georgia and Tennessee. Its 60 towns, with perhaps 20,000 residents, made it the largest tribe in the Southeast. With the coming of the white man, the Cherokee—along with other Southeastern tribes—tried to conform to the white man's civilization. The tribe adopted the white man's dress, set up a new government along Western lines and even owned Negro slaves.

But adoption of many of the white man's ways did not lead to acceptance in the white man's eyes. This became apparent in 1830 when Congress authorized the purchase of Indian lands in the Southeast and removal of Indians to lands beyond the Mississippi River. During the next 16 years the various tribes were uprooted, sometimes by force, and marched to the far-away lands of Oklahoma. Along the infamous "Trail of Tears" the Cherokee, Creeks, Choctaws, Chickasaws and Seminoles carried their few possessions.

The Cherokee, given two years to prepare for the move, resisted expulsion and were forced from their homes by troops. As they marched West in 1838-39, they chanted a song that went like this:

I have no more land.
I am driven away from home,
Driven up the red waters.
Let us all go.
Let us all die together.

Die together many of them did. Of one group of more than 12,000, a third perished along the arduous way. Settled in Oklahoma, the Indian tribes later faced further demands of the white man. The western part of what is now Oklahoma was taken from them after the Civil War, pressing the tribes closer together in eastern Oklahoma.

In recent years the Cherokee, proud of their heritage, have sought to perpetuate the history and culture of their forefathers. A major force in this direction has been the Cherokee National Historical Society, organized in 1963. One of the projects sponsored by the association has been the Oconaluftee Indian Village, intended to depict the history and culture of the red man.

During the great evacuation of Indians, some of the Cherokee refused to make the westward trek, hiding instead in the forests and rocky areas of the Great Smoky Mountains. Their descendants today live on the Qualla Reservation at the edge of Great Smoky Mountains National Park, the

Oconaluftee Indian Village, replica of Indian village of 200 years ago, is a part of the Qualla Indian Reservation at Cherokee, North Carolina

largest Indian reservation east of Wisconsin. It is here you may visit Oconaluftee Indian Village, a replica of an 18th century village, peopled with Cherokee descendants. The village contains five structures of ancient design and an open-air temple where tribal rituals are held. Ringing the compound is a palisade of more than 2000 locust poles which, in an earlier era, protected the community from other tribes and from animals.

The structures include three types of homes in which the Cherokee lived. The oldest reproduction is one in which the walls are of woven river cane over which a plaster of river clay was applied. Other structures are of log construction, including a seven-sided council house. In the council house fireplace was kept the sacred fire of the Cherokee, an eternal flame that was never permitted to burn out. Here, too, are the bows and arrows, the guns, the hand-carved wood masks used in dances and worn by the medicine man in his rituals. Within the compound Indian men and women continue to make pottery, baskets, blowguns and dug-out canoes, practicing techniques that are almost extinct.

NEW ECHOTA

Prior to its expulsion to the West, the Cherokee tribe made a valiant effort to live by the white man's standards by creating New Echota, a remarkable town in Georgia that served as the capital of the Cherokee nation. In the process, the tribe discarded the traditional clan system of rule and devised a republican system of control. It divided its nation into eight districts, represented at a legislature at the new capital.

The town boasted a national newspaper and printing office, legislative hall, supreme court house, mission station and several dwellings and commercial establishments. The newspaper, the *Cherokee Phoenix,* was printed both in English and in Cherokee, utilizing a written form of the Cherokee tongue with symbols representing syllables.

American missionaries played such a role in educating the Cherokee that by 1830 a quarter of the Indians were participating in Christian services. The missionary most closely associated with the new capital was the Reverend Samuel A. Worcester, an emissary of the American Board, Congregationalist, who built himself a home near the capital in 1827.

After the removal of the Cherokee all buildings, with the exception of the Worcester house, were torn down and the land on which they stood was plowed by farmers. All trace of the village was lost until the 1950s when a group of residents in

Newspaper office was a part of New Echota, one-time capital of Cherokees

24

Baking oven at Indian City in Andarko, Oklahoma

nearby Calhoun located the site and bought 220 acres of the original land. The group, hoping for financial aid to recreate the town, deeded the site to the state. The General Assembly provided funds for recreation of the village in 1957, and the Georgia Historical Commission arranged for archaeological excavations to determine the foundation sites of the original buildings. The commission has since restored the Worcester House and recreated the Vann Tavern, the Print Shop and the Court House. It has also built an interpretive museum to help explain the significance of the town. Other structures are being reconstructed as research and excavation uncover their foundations.

TSA-LA-GI

When the Cherokee National Historical Society was formed it made as its principal project the construction of a Cherokee Cultural Center three miles south of Tahlequah, Oklahoma. It was on this site that the old Cherokee nation built seminaries for education and turned out millions of pages of print in both Cherokee and English at its Park Hill Press.

The project includes an outdoor amphitheater where an epic symphonic drama will be presented annually during the summer season, a museum showing the development of the Cherokee from his beginning and an archive. It also includes Tsa-la-gi, a living museum or re-creation of an Indian village as it looked about 1700 to 1750. Since the intent is to recreate the village as it might have been prior to the white man's influence, all materials—clothing, weapons, cooking utensils and basketry—were made in the village in the manner they were fashioned 300 years ago.

Visitors are guided through the village by trained young Cherokee guides, who do all the explaining. The Cherokee "inhabitants," on the other hand, play the role of their forebears of 300 years ago in silence, feigning ignorance of the English tongue.

The village consists of a number of log dwellings plastered with mud, a large log council house and communal areas, all surrounded by a high palisade. Craft demonstrations include the preparation of foods, weaving, pottery, hide tanning and bow, arrow and blowgun making.

INDIAN CITY, U.S.A.

This museum village in Oklahoma, located on 160 acres which formed a part of the Kiowa, Co-

Artifacts excite children at Kicotan Indian Village

manche and Apache reservation, is designed as a vast outdoor museum containing a series of reconstructed Indian villages. It was organized by residents of nearby Andarko to provide visitors with a sampling of the Indian way of life and to give Indians an opportunity to make and sell their wares.

Here, complete with ancient cooking utensils and tools, are seven typical villages representing various periods. One village is that of a nomadic hunting tribe, others of the buffalo-hunting tribes, the Plains Indians. Three houses in the Navajo village show two methods used by the Navajo in building homes.

Most impressive of the villages is that of the Wichita, with its 40-foot-high council house. The women did all of the building in the Wichita tribe, erecting a framework of pine poles and covering this with willow branches and swamp grass.

The tipi was the traveling home of the Kiowa, Comanche and Arapaho tribes, while "earth lodges" depict the Pawnee way of life. Other structures reconstruct the grass-covered wickiups of the Chiricahua Apache, the council house and homes of the Caddo, and the stone house of the Pueblo people.

KICOTAN INDIAN VILLAGE

Long before the English established their first settlement in Virginia in 1607, the Kicotan Indians ruled half of what is now coastal Virginia. The Kicotan (or Kecoughtan), one of the many Algonquin tribes, greeted the English settlers at Hampton and warmly welcomed them to their village. A few years later friendship turned to hostility and the Kicotans were eventually driven off their lands.

To commemorate the brief friendship, the Kecoughtan chapter of the Virginia Archaeological Society decided in 1967 to recreate the Indian village that Captain John Smith knew. The result is a complex of six arched dwellings within a log stockade in the city of Hampton. In the interest of authenticity, mats were hand-sewn to form the outside of the dwellings and tied together by leather thongs. The cured skins, tools fashioned from rocks and various earthenware vessels in the lodges are similar in detail to the originals.

INDIAN VILLAGE

In the Finger Lakes Region of New York, the Owasco Indians settled in small numbers about 100 A.D. and remained the dominant tribe for more than a thousand years. Through these centuries the tribe developed a high degree of culture, refining new techniques in pottery and crafts. The Owasco nation in time spawned the Iroquois League, embracing the Seneca, Cayuga, Onondaga, Mohawk, Oneida and Tuscarora.

Aware of the early importance of the Owasco culture to this region, Professor Walter K. Long, director of the Cayuga Museum of History and Art, conceived the idea of recreating a stockaded village of circa 1050 A.D. near the foot of Owasco Lake, two miles south of Auburn, New York. Local individuals and organizations provided support and backing for the project. Construction of an exhibition lodge was expanded to become a full-fledged village, which opened in 1967.

The village is an authentic reconstruction on a site where previous excavations revealed evidence of Indian dwellings. Within the stockade are early long houses as well as smaller shelters. The long houses, designed for use by as many as 20 families, consisted of a framework of sapling poles covered by bark. They served as home, place of worship, school and community center.

The village is designed to tell you much about the Owasco life. It has within its bounds corn fields, a tobacco patch, a tanning pit where hides were soaked to loosen fur, a bark trough used for storing clay from which pottery was made, one rack set up for drying wood during summer months and another for drying and smoking fish for the months ahead.

A museum adjoining the village has exhibits illustrating the growth of the Owasco culture, emphasizing the development of pottery, hunting and crafts.

Long houses are protected by stockade at Owasco Indian Village

Costumed settlers form a wall at Jamestown Festival Park

3

First Settlements and Colonial Towns

MORE THAN any other country, Spain led the way to colonization of the Americas. In the 16th century she was a great kingdom and an adventurous sea power. Her explorers probed not only the coast but the inland areas of the New World, finding the gold and silver they sought in South America.

England was a rival power, hoping through colonization to divert into her own some of the treasure that poured into Spain's coffers. An early colonist wrote, "We seek new worlds, for gold, for praise, for glory." There is little doubt the highest priority was placed on gold.

England's attempts to secure a foothold on the new continent were unsuccessful in the 16th century. Some colonists endured a number of seasons in the strange land and were thankful to return to Mother England with the arrival of supply ships. A colony on Roanoke Island, North Carolina, vanished completely, the only clue to its disappearance the word "Croatan" engraved in a tree. Lost with this contingent of colonists was Virginia Dare, first English child born in America.

It was something of a miracle that England's first two settlements on the Eastern seaboard survived. Both were short on supplies and ill-prepared to cope with the new climate and the virgin land. Disease and starvation decimated the ranks of colonists at both Jamestown, Virginia, and Plymouth, Massachusetts, nearly adding two more names to the list of English colonies founded in hope and abandoned in despair.

To found Jamestown, three ships—the 100-ton *Susan Constant,* the 40-ton *Godspeed,* and the 20-ton *Discoverer*—sailed from London on December 20, 1606. It was the hope of their captain, Christopher Newport, that the voyage would take no longer than four months, making possible an early spring planting in the New World.

The ships anchored at Chesapeake Bay on Sunday, April 26, 1607. After exploring a broad river, the colonists on May 13 chose a wooded peninsula some 30 miles from the sea as their new home and named both river and town after King James. From the first the hostility of Indians made life more unendurable. This called for the quick construction of a fort.

Colonist George Percy wrote, "The fifteenth of June, we had built and finished our Fort, which was triangle-wise, having three Bulwarkes at every corner, like a halfe moone, and foure or five pieces of artillerie mounted in them." The fort and structures within them were built by dwindling numbers of men. Plagued by malaria and famine, the 144 colonists who had set out with optimism were 38 in number when supplies were replenished by a ship in January, 1608.

With similar planning to avoid famine, the *Mayflower*, with 102 colonists, was scheduled to sail from England in April, 1620, early enough to plant a first crop for fall harvest in America. For reasons of supply, weather and caprice, the sailing was delayed until August, and it was on cold and winter-barren land that the Pilgrims landed, first at Provincetown at the tip of Cape Cod and then at Plymouth, on December 20.

Governor William Bradford noted in his journal, "That which was most sad and lamentable was, that in two or three months' time half of their company died, especially in January and February, being the depth of winter, and wanting houses and other comforts; being infected with the scurvy and other diseases which this long voyage and their inaccommodate condition had brought upon them."

Both settlements survived, prospered, and spawned others. The precarious existence became a full and comfortable life. The first clusters of purely functional dwellings became solid and architecturally refined structures on well-ordered streets. A visit to the two first settlements, now recreated, will contrast sharply with a visit to the later colonial villages open to the public along the Eastern Coast.

JAMESTOWN, VIRGINIA

History credits Captain John Smith, a soldier of fortune, with a major role in the survival of Jamestown. It was he, elected by the colonists' council to head the settlement, who ordered and supervised construction of the first tiny huts within the stockade. He bolstered the fort, organized parties for trade with the Indians and foraged for food. One of his dictates was that "he that will not work shall not eat, except by sickness he be disabled."

The stockade enclosed a church, storehouse, guardhouse and fifteen houses. Five years after it was founded the colony gained an economic base by planting and curing sweet tobacco for export to England. Peace with the Indians prompted settlers to build new homes outside the fort, and the town of Jamestown was well on its way.

When no longer useful, the stockaded fort with its wattle-and-daub homes was demolished. It

Aerial view shows
reconstructed James Fort

Corn grows tall near blockhouse at Plimoth Plantation

remained nothing more than descriptive passages in old journals and fairly complete depictions in ancient drawings until the State of Virginia began to plan its 350th anniversary celebration.

The eight-month celebration, which opened on April 1, 1957, was preceded by a number of Herculean tasks, including the re-creation of Jamestown's first settlement, of the three ships which brought the first colonists and of various structures which played an important part in the survival of the colony. All this is on permanent exhibit today at Jamestown Festival Park, operated by the National Park Service. Your tour will begin at a visitor center which houses half a million Jamestown artifacts, uncovered by the Park Service during archaeological work. Here, too, are film programs and dioramas, providing an orientation to Jamestown life as it progressed.

Among new settlers in the first years were eight Germans and Poles, brought over to produce glass. In addition to the excavated site of the 1608 glasshouse, the Park Service has recreated a glass factory, duplicating in layout and techniques the manner in which that craft was introduced.

Paying tribute to the part which the more friendly Indians played in Jamestown's history is a reconstruction of Chief Powhatan's lodge, with its framework of saplings and its cover of cattail leaves.

But the prizes for visitors are the re-creation of James Fort and the three ships which were the symbols of the Jamestown Festival. The 18 buildings within the stockaded fort, all authentically furnished, were built of Virginia hardwood held together with wooden trunnels in place of nails and covered with woven grapevines and mud. The replicas of the *Susan Constant,* the *Godspeed,* and the *Discovery* conform in tonnage, size and type with all known information about the Jamestown ships.

Within the area is a stone tablet which appropriately reads: *"At Jamestown began: the expansion overseas of the English-speaking peoples; the Commonwealth of Virginia; the United States of America; and the British Commonwealth of Nations."*

PLYMOUTH, MASSACHUSETTS

In no other town in the country does the Pilgrim story, the founding of America story, come through as it does in this community south of Boston. This is Pilgrim country, history country, legend country, its weathered houses and fine museums speaking eloquently of New England's beginning, of what our forefathers endured to make today's life possible. That portion of the seafront which the Pilgrims knew so well has been largely set aside in a number of ways to commemorate the Pilgrim story.

The Pilgrim National Monument is a hilltop park, offering a fine view of the sea and of the islands the Pilgrims explored after their landing. A short distance away, the rock on which the Pilgrims stepped from their shallop to reach shore is enshrined in an opensided marble edifice. A few steps away is First House and 1627 House, re-created examples of Pilgrim houses of 1620 and 1627.

Across the street is Cole's Hill, where the Pilgrims laid to rest their dead in the winter of 1620-21. On the crest of the hill stands a bronze statue of Massasoit, chief of the Wampanoag Indians, and a granite sarcophagus containing the remains of many Pilgrims. Nearby, too, during the warm weather months is *Mayflower II,* the full-scale replica of the ship that brought the Pilgrims to Plymouth. It was built for Plimoth Plantation at Brixham, England, and sailed across the Atlantic on its maiden voyage under the command of Captain Alan Villiers, a crossing of 53 days.

Three miles south of this historic area is Plimoth Plantation, a re-creation of the Pilgrim village of 1627. The Pilgrims called their plantation a "new planting," and Governor Bradford prophetically said, "As one small candle may light a thousand, so the light here kindled has shown to many, yea in some sorte to our whole nation."

By 1627 the community was reasonably sure of success. From this small settlement, colonists soon broke out and established new towns in the Colony of New Plymouth—Duxbury, Scituate, Taunton, Yarmouth, Barnstable. They produced what they could for their needs and traded furs, clapboard and other products of the new world to pay for their necessary imports.

The modern Plimoth Plantation has re-created this community, using old records, eyewitness accounts of visitors to the original colony, archaeological research and the history written by their leader, William Bradford.

When you visit it, you will find a functioning village in which guides and hostesses in Pilgrim dress carry on the tasks necessary for living in a 17th century farming community. They will inter-

Simple houses reflect early life at Pioneer Village in Salem, Massachusetts

rupt their work to answer your questions and sometimes let you try your hand at some of the 17th century household skills. You may find sheep and chickens wandering loose in the village and men at work cutting planks in a pine grove or splitting shingles. The intent is to heighten the illusion of reality and to offer the visitor, through dialogue and activity, a fuller understanding of Pilgrim life.

To this end, each house places its emphasis on one facet of Pilgrim life. The emphasis is on cooking in the Warren House, the military in the Myles Standish House, the intellectual and cultural in the Brewster House.

The plantation has long-range plans for expansion. Close by the village is an Indian campsite where you may inspect the bark houses occupied by the Pilgrims' Indian friends. Planned are the reconstruction of an Indian village as it might have been before the arrival of the white man and exhibits to tell the story of the colony during the six decades from 1630 until it was absorbed by Massachusetts Bay in 1692.

SALEM, MASSACHUSETTS

Smaller in size than Plimoth Plantation is Pioneers' Village in Salem, north of Boston. The reproduction of Salem of 1630, as Squire John Winthrop knew it after his landing in that year, was established in 1930 by the city as a part of the observance of the 300th anniversary of the founding of Massachusetts.

The village admirably depicts a transitional period in the lives of the first settlers. Sod-roofed dugouts of palisaded logs and bark-covered wigwams illustrate the shelters first used while planks were being hewn in a log pit for more permanent construction. By way of contrast, the nearby pine cottages with their thatch roofs and catted chimneys of log and clay are typical of the homes the settlers left in England. Scattered throughout the village are such industrial exhibits as an apparatus for making salt from sea water, a brick kiln, the fish flakes and the pit for sawing logs.

WILLIAMSBURG, VIRGINIA

While Plymouth remained a comparatively small community, Jamestown achieved greatness as Virginia's cultural, social and legislative center. Unfortunately, the State House at Jamestown appeared susceptible to fire. When the fourth State House suffered the same fate as its predecessors by burning to the ground in 1698, the Virginia General Assembly moved the capital to Middle Plantation six miles inland and renamed the village Williamsburg in honor of King William III.

The new capital soon burgeoned into Virginia's chief village. It was a planned community, following a design drawn by Governor Francis Nicholson. The winding main road was straightened and named for the Duke of Gloucester, the Capitol placed at the eastern end of the avenue facing the College of William and Mary and the village divided into half-acre lots on which dwellings were set back by law six feet from the street. In this new Capitol, Patrick Henry spoke out for freedom, and George Washington and James Madison began their legislative careers.

For 80 years, Williamsburg ranked as high in the colonies as such sophisticated centers as Boston, Philadelphia, New York and Newport. Its growth as a regional center was curbed in 1779, in the same way as that of Jamestown, when the state government moved to Richmond. At its height, Williamsburg was envied for its wealth, culture and architecture. Through the years the gems of architecture and the glories of the past lost their luster as the community settled into a lesser role as county seat and college town.

The grandeur that was Colonial Williamsburg might have been lost excepting for the dream of restoration nurtured by the Reverend Dr. W.A.R. Goodwin, a dream turned into reality by John D. Rockefeller Jr. Rockefeller's purpose, when he began the gigantic restoration in 1926, was "to re-create accurately the environment of men and women of 18th century Williamsburg and to bring about such an understanding of their lives and times that present and future generations may more vividly appreciate the contribution of these early Americans to the ideals and culture of our country."

Within the 130-acre historic area there are more than 80 original 18th century structures and ninety gardens. Meticulous research went into each of more than a hundred buildings to determine their history, their early appearance and their exact furnishings. Large sums of money were spent to locate on this continent and in Europe the old, authentic treasures and to return them to their proper setting. The same concern for authenticity extended to a program of crafts, which has grown to a point where more than 30 are demonstrated by skilled artisans using tools and implements of more than 200 years ago.

A visit to Williamsburg begins at an Information Center where you are briefed by a film, "Williamsburg, The Story of a Patriot," on the history

Tall trees line main thoroughfare at Colonial Williamsburg

and significance of the area. You are then free to wander the broad streets and inspect such structures as the gaol, which once held captive Blackbeard's pirate crew, and the Golden Ball where once again a silversmith practices his exacting craft.

The reconstructed Capitol, with its rounded, arched windows and its tall hexagonal cupola, is much as it was when Virginia legislators adopted a Resolution for American Independence without a dissenting voice. In 1953 President Eisenhower stood by the original speaker's chair and said, "I think no American could stand in these halls and on this spot without feeling a very great and deep sense of the debt we owe to the courage, the stamina, and the faith of our forefathers."

George Washington's diaries mention 30 visits to Henry Wetherburn's Tavern. Lafayette enjoyed a tumultuous welcome on his return to Williamsburg in 1824, an event which was capped by a stately banquet in the Raleigh Tavern. The state's first two governors, Patrick Henry and Thomas Jefferson, had as their official residence the Governor's Palace, a dignified brick structure which

in the colonial era was the home of seven royal governors.

But Williamsburg is more than names and history. It is a visual delight in which the solidity of brick or frame structure is set off by broad greens and unexpected gardens. It is a community that is never static, where horse-drawn carriages roll along Duke of Gloucester Street and the air is occasionally filled with the martial music of a costumed fife and drum corps. During his lifetime, Rockefeller said, "You can't appreciate Williamsburg unless you walk through the town. Always you see something different, a fence or a chimney from some angle you never saw before."

The scope of Colonial Williamsburg is constantly being broadened. Its expansion has included the acquisition of additional historic buildings in the adjacent area, along with select examples of early English and American furnishings. It offers a year-round program with such events as antique forums and seminars on preservation and restoration. Colonial Williamsburg, America's first major restoration, remains among the best of them.

Costumed craftsmen use early methods at Williamsburg

PORTSMOUTH, NEW HAMPSHIRE

The history of Portsmouth began in 1630 with the arrival of a sea-battered sailing ship in the mouth of the Piscataqua River. What attracted the eyes of the colonists, starved for fresh fruit after a two-month voyage, was a hillside crimson with wild strawberries. The colonists landed to reap the unexpected harvest and, impressed by the inlet, decided to make it their home. The settlement of Strawbery Banke began with a concentration of buildings around Puddle Dock. Wharves were built on timber pilings and about these were clustered the shops and homes of merchants, shipbuilders, cabinetmakers and other craftsmen.

As Portsmouth grew, the demand for prime land was such that Puddle Dock was filled in to become the site for new homes and new shops. It is on 10 acres of both sides of what was Puddle Dock that Strawbery Banke, a village restoration, now stands.

It will be some years before Puddle Dock is returned to its original inlet status, complete with the structures and activities that brought it wealth. But standing today on both sides of it are re-minders of Portsmouth's former glory, tracing the growth of the town and its historical significance. Here you may reach an understanding of life as it was in colonial America and of life in the early years of the new Republic.

On one side of Puddle Dock are buildings which the colonists knew well more than 200 years ago. In the three-story Chase House (1762) George Washington was entertained by Stephen Chase in 1789. In the Joseph Sherbourne House, circa 1660, visitors once had a fine view of the ships which lined the docks. And in the Captain John Clark House (1750) expanding commerce was undoubtedly a frequent topic of conversation.

The other side of Puddle Dock recaptures later episodes in the city's history. Here are important landmarks moved from other parts of Portsmouth for restoration. These include Stoodley's Tavern, circa 1765; the Daniel Webster House (1786), and the Governor Goodwin Mansion (1811), restored residence of the state's first Civil War governor.

These were among the scores of fine old structures which lost much of their glamor as they merged with newer homes and shops along the

Dunaway General Store at Strawbery Banke, New Hampshire

Exterior and interior of Governor Goodwin Mansion

crowded streets of downtown Portsmouth. It was the imminence of urban renewal that led to their restoration. City plans in 1957 called for leveling the Puddle Dock area in order to erect garden-type apartments. A group of citizens, inspired by Miss Dorothy Vaughn, a librarian and historian, formed Strawbery Banke, Inc., in an effort to save those homes rich in history and architecture. The organization persuaded the Urban Renewal Administration to make this a pilot program in restoration, gaining $650,000 in federal funds to clear the area and to relocate residents. The city contributed another $150,000. The corporation supervised the removal of junk yards, weedy back alleys and structures without historical value. It retained 27 old homes on their original foundations, carefully stripped away later embellishments and restored them to their early state.

Today, costumed guides will take you along wide streets and period gardens into buildings which will give you an insight into the unique character of Portsmouth houses and the people who lived in them. At Strawbery Banke you may judge the extent of changes in American villages during a span of two centuries.

ST. AUGUSTINE, FLORIDA

Spain was not only a pioneer in probing the southern portion of North America but a persistent pioneer. Juan Ponce de Leon, Spanish governor of Puerto Rico, explored the entire coast of Florida in 1513, hoping to find treasure and a fountain or river which could transform old age into youth. Other Spanish emissaries tried unsuccessfully to colonize Florida. Pedro Menendez, a distinguished naval commander, in 1565 founded St. Augustine and established a series of military posts from Tampa Bay to Santa Elena in South Carolina.

Like Old Deerfield in Massachusetts, a portion of historic St. Augustine is a museum village which is a living restoration. The restored area remains a part of the greater city. However, structures within its boundaries which do not belong to the early period have been removed and such telltale signs of our time as light poles and television antennas have been eliminated. In buildings returned to their old luster people live as homeowners or tenants and work as shopkeepers or craftsmen.

The 20-year restoration project, now past its mid-point, aims at returning the old Spanish quarter to its appearance in the 18th century, when the original military post had grown considerably and had developed an identity of its own among Spain's colonies. The life of colonial Spain is renewed in shops which are interspersed among privately owned homes. Within the shops, costumed craftsmen demonstrate crafts and sell products which follow the Spanish tradition of 1565-1763 and of the second period of Spanish possession of St. Augustine from 1783 to 1821.

Spain's early determination to maintain its colony is dramatized by the Castillo de San Marcos, St. Augustine's fortress. Its 20th century wish to share Hispanic culture is expressed in an exhibition building it constructed and maintains within the restored village. The Castillo de San Marcos, oldest masonry fort in the nation, was meant to be impregnable. Workmen labored almost 25

*Old Spain comes alive
at Castillo de San Marcos*

39

Ancient wooden schoolhouse is part of St. Augustine restoration

years from 1672 to 1696 building walls that rise 30 feet and are up to 12 feet thick. A 40-foot moat was built around the elaborate four-bastioned stronghold.

The fort, attacked by pirates, Indians and Englishmen but never captured, is today a national monument administered by the National Park Service. Visitors cross the drawbridge and take a guided tour by audio devices. From the ramparts they have a far view of the city and the bay.

Spain's more recent contribution, as part of the restoration program, was construction of Casa del Hidalgo, a Spanish cultural center and tourist information office. The Casa is a complex including a house museum, a carriage wing and a dormitory for servants. The buildings, which conform to 17th century Spanish architecture, house Spanish antiques and special exhibits.

These are incidentals to the overall restoration program which began in 1959 with an appropriation of $150,000 by the Florida legislature to establish a St. Augustine Historical Restoration and Preservation Commission. The master plan of the commission stated, "It shall be the objective of this commission to obtain, with its own resources and those of others, as nearly accurate as possible a restoration of the ancient walled city of St. Augustine. Recognizing that this area includes the present business heart of the modern city, and that the ultimate sources of funds to accomplish its objectives are as yet uncertain, the commission proposes to divide its project into a

St. Augustine's Oldest House has Spanish and English features

series of stages, which may be approached over a succession of years to minimize any possible unfavorable impact on local business interests." The commission decided that "where preservation can be accomplished, it shall take the precedence over restoration; where restoration can be accomplished, it will take precedence over reconstruction. Where historic buildings have disappeared, but re-creation of the historic environment is deemed important, they shall be reconstructed in the form and on the site they originally existed."

The project began with restoration of the Arrivas House, now headquarters for the commission, and reconstruction of two completely different types of Spanish residences. It continued with the support of citizens who restored their homes, follow-

ing guidelines established by the commission and with the support of the United States and Latin American countries.

Today, the colonial days of St. Augustine have been revived in five areas, including a mission area outside the city. The main thrust of restoration has been in Calle Real, an area behind the ancient city gates where you may find demonstrating craft shops, Spanish residences and other structures typifying the colony of the 18th century.

In other restoration areas are such buildings as St. Augustine's Oldest House, which evolved from the 17th century to a charming stucco residence with Spanish and old English features, and the Fernandez-Llambias House, restored and furnished as a memorial to Minorcan colonists.

4

Life in the New Republic

WITH THE EXCITING FREEDOM which came with victory in the Revolutionary War, the character of American life began to assume its own unique personality. The new nation was comparatively isolated by distance and time of travel from the countries of Europe. Its financial well-being depended on successful trade and competition with other nations. And compete it did.

American ships took on new designs and, aided by a vast supply of timber, a new sturdiness. Industry drew on a wealth of natural resources to lessen a dependence on European supplies and to bring in needed revenue from the world market. The fertile lands produced a bountiful harvest, much of it for export.

In the remaining years of the 18th century and through the formative years of the 19th century the United States flexed its muscles and tested its strength. It experimented with new forms of art, architecture and literature. It established a way of life, described with much distaste by such European writers as Mrs. Frances Trollope and with predictions of greatness by others such as Alexis de Tocqueville.

These are the winds of change which you may feel in a good number of museum villages in the lands east of the Mississippi. Beginning in the Northeast with New England, here are some of the major ones.

SHELBURNE, VERMONT

Those with an affection for the best and the most unusual objects related to early American life regard Shelburne Museum as the champagne of American villages. It is an intoxicating mixture of the expected and totally unexpected in Americana. It has the added bonus of contrasting this with the finest of European art and antiques of identical periods.

Shelburne Museum, with its diversity and excellent taste, is a tribute to its founder, Mrs. Electra Havemeyer Webb. It is not an authentic village, nor does it represent itself as such. Rather, it is a gathering of many structures, rescued from probable destruction in their original settings and now depicting with gemlike quality the best and most nostalgic aspects of America's past.

As a child, Electra Havemeyer, daughter of sugar millionaire Henry O. Havemeyer, collected antique dolls and doll houses. As she grew older her interest and collection expanded to embrace other areas in the American antiques field. She later wrote, *"How well I recall my mother, Mrs. Henry O. Havemeyer, saying, 'How can you, who*

Entrance, Shelburne Museum

have been brought up with Rembrandts and Manets, collect and live with such American trash?' She was referring to some folk art sculpture I had already started to collect at a very early age and which I loved just as much as she did her fine collections of European art.

"Obviously my mother did not consider my eagles, cigar store Indians, and primitive furniture art at all, which brings us to the matter of individual taste and to a suitable definition of art, particularly folk art."

Miss Havemeyer's enthusiasm was such that she continued to add hundreds of pieces to her antiques collection after her marriage in 1910 to J. Watson Webb, great-grandson of Cornelius Vanderbilt. By 1947 her collection contained more than 125,000 objects.

The Webbs lived in Manhattan for much of the year and spent summer months in their home at Shelburne. Webb, a native Vermonter, was the son of parents who were lifelong residents of Burlington and Shelburne. It was at Shelburne that Mrs. Webb decided to create a museum and bought eight acres of land, including one house, close by the shores of Lake Champlain.

Just as her collection began with dolls and went on to encompass many specialties, her museum began with one building and went on to encompass many period structures, all brimming with priceless objects. The original building, now known as the Variety Unit, was restored and redecorated to house her collection of pewter, ceramics, glass, dolls and doll houses. The Horseshoe Barn, built from hand-hewn timbers some 60 feet long and taken from 11 old barns in the area, contains a collection of more than 200 carriages, sleighs and coaches.

Early Vermont is much in evidence at the dignified Charlotte Meeting House, completely furnished with altars, pews, prayer books and stoves from the Miltonboro Church. Its Stagecoach Inn, built by Captain Hezekiah Barnes in Charlotte, Vermont, in 1783, became vacant in 1948 after use as a home by many families. It was carefully dismantled, timber by timber and brick by brick, and re-erected at Shelburne. This was a job which, among other things, meant rebuilding ten chimneys with roughly 40,000 bricks.

Mrs. Webb's discriminating eye for the best in Americana was not blind to structures other than homes. The 168-foot double-lane covered bridge, which now connects the major highway with the museum, was due to be replaced in Cambridge, 35 miles away, after service as a span across the

Lamoille River for more than a hundred years. Mrs. Webb acquired it and had it brought, timber by timber, to its present location.

The same concern brought about a relocation of other structures, like the Colchester Lighthouse, built in 1871 in the middle of Lake Champlain. It extended beyond buildings to the *S.S. Ticonderoga,* the last surviving sidewheel steamboat built in the grand American tradition. The steamboat, 220 feet long, was moved 9000 feet overland to its present site near the lighthouse.

Today, within its 45 acres, the museum is a unique collection of 35 buildings, depicting three centuries of American life. Some of its homes are furnished to depict the manner in which families lived in yesteryear. Other buildings are appropriate settings for collections of such objects as figureheads, weathervanes, trade signs and toys. A goodly share of the artifacts on display includes Chinese export ware, German toys, European art and objects of foreign origin. While some museum villages limit themselves to their own area, Shelburne covers New England and far regions beyond it.

DEERFIELD, MASSACHUSETTS

Deerfield, located in rolling country west of the Connecticut River, was the most westerly town in Massachusetts when it was settled in the 1660s. It was destroyed by Indians in 1675 during King Philip's War. A second attack and massacre leveled half the town during Queen Anne's War in 1704, when Indians slaughtered 49 persons and marched more than a hundred others to Canada as captives.

Curiously, it was this disastrous episode in the town's history that led in later years to the preservation of Old Deerfield and its position as a pioneer in the preservation and restoration movement. Indian House, a building which had survived an assault by arrows and tomahawks in 1704, was scheduled to be razed in 1847 to make way for a more substantial structure. Residents who regarded it as historically important organized a fund drive for its preservation. While the fund drive fell short of its goal, it gained significance as the first organized attempt at preservation in New England and one of the first in the country. The house was demolished but portions of it were rescued and are now exhibited in the town's famed museum, Memorial Hall.

Through the years the town was fortunate in having a number of persons concerned about preservation. Foremost among these was George Sheldon, a scholar and lecturer who amassed a huge collection of furnishings, artifacts and papers

General store is one of 35 buildings at Shelburne

Steamboat, S. S. Ticonderoga, rests proudly at Shelburne

dealing with Deerfield's early history. Sheldon, who died in 1916, was a leader in forming a historical society, the Pocumtuck Valley Memorial Association, in 1870. The society acquired Memorial Hall for use as a museum and library. It also acquired Frary House, an early salt-box, and furnished it in period.

The cause of restoration and preservation was taken up in the 1940s by Henry N. Flynt of Greenwich, Connecticut, an attorney and a trustee of Deerfield Academy, which is located in the heart of the town. Flynt, with the enthusiastic support of his wife, acquired the old Deerfield Inn. The couple restored the building, furnished it with antiques and began to acquire other significant structures. Before they were through, they were responsible for the restoration of more than 25 buildings. As part of their work the couple established the Heritage Foundation, which maintains 10 historic homes, furnished in period and open to the public. With the support of Deerfield Academy and the Memorial Association, Flynt achieved his objective. This was to create not an antiquarian restoration of any period but an old and charming town center in which residents continue to live, teach and learn.

Today, if you enter Deerfield from the north,

you round a bend and find before you a mile-long stretch of houses, most of them predating the Revolution. The street, described by some as the most beautiful in New England, has been designated as a National Historic Site. It represents the restoration of a complete village, its buildings spanning the period from the 17th to the 20th century.

The commercial impact of this century has been masked in many ways. There is an absence of gasoline stations, neon signs and billboards. Electric and telephone wires are installed underground. The only store is a gift shop housed in an ell of Hall Tavern, which was restored and furnished in the period of the late 17th and early 18th centuries. Even the comparatively new post office has an old look. It reflects the original design of the Third Meeting House of Deerfield, which served the village from 1696 to 1728.

A stroll along Village Street will take you past 25 pre-Revolutionary houses, some of them open to the public. It will also take you past the White Church, a Greek Revival edifice erected in 1838, and the Brick Church, built in 1824. In line with the concept of making the town a living museum, Flynt acquired the White Church and turned it into a community center and Sunday school.

STURBRIDGE, MASSACHUSETTS

During the first half of the 19th century, more than 80 per cent of the New England population lived in country towns. These communities had in common a village green, dominated by a tall-spired, white-painted church and rimmed by such functional structures as a village inn and a country store.

A village resident of that era would feel completely at home at Old Sturbridge Village, a re-creation of a New England community reflecting American rural life in the period from 1790 to 1840. The village has some 40 exhibit buildings, brought together from various parts of New England and complementing each other to form a unified entity.

All buildings on the 1200-acre site are staffed by hosts, hostesses or demonstrating craftsmen wearing the floor-length Empire gowns and homespun shirts of the period. Crafts are practiced daily in such buildings as the farmhouse, printing office and pottery shop.

The center of the village is the green, or common, where during summer months you may hear a troubadour singing early ballads. At one end of the common is the Baptist Meetinghouse, built in Sturbridge in 1832 and an early example of the Greek Revival architectural style. Facing it at the opposite end is the imposing General Salem Towne mansion, erected in Charlton in 1794. The variety of houses is such that you may trace the refinement in home design from the early Colonial salt-box to the spacious and light-scaled Federal residence with its luxurious ornamentation. In contrast to the more elegant buildings is Miner Grant's unpainted General Store, where you may

Sheep are part of farm family at Old Sturbridge Village

still purchase penny candy, and the solid granite edifice that is Moses Wilder's Blacksmith Shop.

The village has come a long way since it was conceived by Albert B. Wells and J. Cheney Wells, members of a family prominent in central New England for generations. Both men were ardent and discriminating collectors of American antiques and chose the village concept as a means of housing and displaying their collection to the best advantage.

Scholarly research and expansion, continuous from the village opening in 1946, have progressed to a point where the village is a national authority on construction, furnishings and other details of early America.

The expansion in recent years has been concentrated on historical agriculture. The physical plant and activities at the Pliny Freeman Farm, one of the exhibit areas, have been broadened to conduct "live" demonstrations of the daily chores performed by the farmer of 150 years ago. Land is ploughed, tilled, planted and threshed with early implements. Fruit varieties of the early 19th century ripen in the orchards. Farm animals wander freely in the farm compound.

Next step in the expansion will be the re-creation of a manufacturing village. The new complex, centered around a water-powered cotton mill and a clock factory, will have such related structures as a boarding house, mill owner's house, meetinghouse, school and tavern.

WEST SPRINGFIELD, MASSACHUSETTS

Less imposing but charming in its own way is Storrowtown Village on the grounds of the Eastern States Exposition, which sponsors a giant fair, largest in the Northeast, during two weeks in September.

Here 12 buildings represent an authentic New England village dating from 1767 to 1838. Like Old Sturbridge, the buildings are clustered about a green. Unlike Old Sturbridge, the emphasis inside the structures is on antiques and craft objects which are on sale. The range of exhibits and activities, including craft demonstrations, is greatest during the days the Exposition is open.

The village had its beginning in 1926 when the late Mrs. Helen O. Storrow, a Boston philanthropist and an Exposition trustee, bought the Gilbert Homestead, built by a forebear in West Brookfield, Massachusetts, in 1794. Mrs. Storrow decided to make the home the nucleus of a re-created village. She paid $200 for the structure and $10,000 to have it taken down in numbered sec-

tions and reassembled in a corner of the Exposition grounds. Other fine old buildings, including a meeting house, general store, school and tavern, were transplanted from other towns throughout New England.

One of Mrs. Storrow's objectives was to provide permanent buildings for the Exposition's Home Department exhibits. It was her belief that the exhibits, which reflected such early American skills as quilting and crewelwork, would be enhanced by a natural period setting. It was for this purpose the buildings were principally used after Mrs. Storrow donated them to the Exposition in 1929.

Early in 1966, a group of volunteers organized to open the village during warm-weather months as a museum. Today, hostesses in colonial dress provide background information on each building.

Meetinghouse at Old Sturbridge Village

Old ships with tall masts dominate Mystic Seaport skyline

MYSTIC SEAPORT, CONNECTICUT

In the quiet of the morning at Mystic Seaport, on the east bank of the Mystic River ten miles east of New London, you can visualize sharply how it must have been in the good, old days of whaleships and clippers.

You enter the gates of this 37-acre reproduction of a 19th century New England coastal village and the tall masts beckon above the complex of buildings before you.

Here is the whaleship *Charles W. Morgan,* built in 1841; the *Dorothy A. Parsons,* a sailship used for oystering; the *Joseph W. Conrad,* a 100-foot full-rigged vessel which sailed around the world under three flags; and the *L. A. Dunton,* a Gloucester fishing schooner. These are among the historically significant ships and the more than 100 small craft at the seaport, offering an insight into America's skill in fashioning and sailing ships.

But the village is more than a repository of ships. Historic homes, exhibit buildings and craft shops line the cobblestone streets. Its more than 60 major buildings present not only a graphic account of American maritime life but of man's conquest of the sea from the beginning. In the three-story brick Stillman Building, the cornerstone of the formal museum complex, there are rigged ship models, builders' half models, paintings, prints and memorabilia, tracing the development of sailing craft from ingenious Egyptian river boats which sailed the Nile centuries before Cleopatra was born.

Those buildings which deal with one or more facets of shipbuilding and outfitting are meticulously maintained in the appropriate early American period. Here is the Plymouth Cordage Company's 250-foot segment of a ropewalk, built in 1824 and acquired by the seaport association in 1951. In the Nantucket Cooperage, one of the seaport's interpretive corps of 50 persons demonstrates the early process of making casks. Other specialized buildings are devoted to ship carving, weaving, shipsmithing and sailmaking. A portion of the grounds is a working exhibit of shipbuilding where staff members repair and restore the small vessels of the exhibition fleet.

The seaport owes its existence to the Marine Historical Association, founded in 1929 by three area residents who were distressed by the indiscriminate destruction of irreplaceable relics and data dealing with early America's maritime life. The association filled two museum buildings with maritime collections before it acquired the sandbagger *Annie* as its first vessel in 1931. The *Annie,*

a racing sloop built in Mystic in 1880, maintained her stability in competition by having her crew move 30 50-pound bags of sand on each tack.

Expansion from this point was rapid. To provide an appropriate setting for shipbuilding activities and old ships, the association created streets and buildings. In addition to restored structures, the association introduced formal museum buildings to display thousands of models, implements, ship figureheads and scrimshaw pieces.

An aim of the association was to imbue in the youth of America "the spirit of the sea and all for which it stands." To this end, it has provided buildings and exhibits with a special appeal for the young. A Junior Museum has child-height cases with exhibits of seashells, diving equipment and scrimshaw. In the outside play area there is a ship's bridge on which youngsters may take a turn at the wheel and look down the river through binoculars.

The association provides tours for groups of school children, scout troops, and other organizations of young people. It also encourages science classes to visit its planetarium.

RICHMONDTOWN, NEW YORK

Thousands of visitors to New York take one of the world's greatest ferry bargains, the nickel ride through Manhattan's harbor to Staten Island. Those who return without exploring the island are passing up a view of a major village restoration.

This is Richmondtown Restoration, the re-creation of a typical American village of the 17th, 18th and 19th centuries. The multi-million dollar project on 98 acres is sponsored by the Staten Island Historical Society and the City of New York's Department of Parks. The intent is to show in buildings, furnishings, tools, orchards and gardens the simple way of life that gradually developed into our complex modern urban society.

Heart of the restoration is a village settled in the late 1600s and once called Cocclestown. The village grew into the thriving county seat of Richmondtown. In 1898 its growth was halted abruptly when Staten Island became a part of Greater New York and the county seat was moved elsewhere.

The restoration project was conceived by the Staten Island Historical Society in 1932 when it acquired the former county clerk and surrogate's office for its headquarters. A first, small step was the restoration and opening of the Voorlezer's House, built by the Dutch about 1696 as a school, church, and the home of the congregation's schoolteacher and lay reader.

The acquisition of other buildings was gradual until 1952 when the Department of Parks joined forces with the society to buy 98 acres, including the village, and to annex it to an adjacent park. Private tenants evacuated the village, and modern buildings were demolished. Planning, research and construction of a scale model of the reconstruction were financed by a grant from the New York Foundation. Funds were raised to move and restore a number of buildings. Other buildings were moved by the Park Department. The Triborough Bridge and Tunnel Authority authorized $250,000 for construction of a parking area, the re-creation of a saw mill, and the development of the surrounding area.

The village today is concentrated about five streets, along which the story of the development of a town and of the changing life of its people is told through 31 major buildings. Some are restorations. Among them are the Treasure House (1700), so called from the discovery many years ago of some gold coins hidden within its walls; the Stephens General Store (1837), operated as a store for nearly a century, and the Simon Swaim House (circa 1760), a farmhouse with outbuildings.

Other structures either have been or will be rebuilt. These include the Cuckoldstown Inn (circa 1755), the most famous island tavern of its day, the James Fitchett Blacksmith Shop (circa 1700), where generations of the Dubois family worked as smithies, and the Dutch Reformed Church (circa 1768), destroyed by the British during the Revolution as a rebel church.

COOPERSTOWN, NEW YORK

A remarkable complex of three related museums is a tribute to the imagination and foresight of the New York State Historical Association, which conceived and maintains them. The museums are Fenimore House, the Farmers' Museum, and its Village Crossroads.

Fenimore House, headquarters for the association, is noted for its collection of American folk art. Its works include many by painters who improved their native sense of design in the shops of wood carvers and tinsmiths. The art ranges beyond canvas and paper to wood carving, metalwork, needlework, and scrimshaw.

What you see here will give you a better understanding of the nearby Farmers' Museum and its Village Crossroads, which reflect the life of average people in rural New York between 1783 and the 1840s.

The Farmers' Museum is a stone dairy barn, converted into an indoor museum. It houses implements and possessions, most of them handmade, of the average pioneer family. It also permits you to witness, by demonstration, how the implements were used. Beyond the barn, you may wander about a dozen buildings, brought together from a 100-mile area to form the re-created village on a six-acre tract. You may savor the flavor of early rural life at Lippitt Homestead (1797), where flax and broom corn are grown and representative farm animals have the run of the yard. The heart of the house is the busy kitchen where food is cooked, butter churned and chores done as they were from 1800 to 1820. Bump Tavern (circa 1800) is equipped with barroom, ladies' parlor, gentlemen's reading room, ballroom and bedrooms. Other specialized buildings are the doctor's office (1829), druggist's shop (1832), schoolhouse (1810) and printing office (1829).

For those who like to share a hoax which hoodwinked a gullible public in 1869, the village has on display the Cardiff Giant. This was the stone sculpture of a man more than ten feet tall and weighing nearly 3000 pounds which two practical jokers claimed was a petrified giant they had dug from the earth.

MONROE, NEW YORK

What the Farmers' Museum does for rural life, the Old Museum Village of Smith's Clove does for the evolution of industry in America. It traces the manner in which goods were produced from the homespun era through the craft shop period and into today's reliance on mechanized industry.

The 36-building complex around a village green was the brainchild of Roscoe W. Smith, founder of the Orange and Rockland Electric Company of Monroe, New York. Smith became aware in 1915 that tools which led to the industrial revolution were being discarded. He embarked on his own crusade to collect and preserve them. At about the same time his wife declared her intention to collect early glass, china and other antiques.

The couple toured the countryside through the years, amassing so many objects that they required special storage. A wish to display the collection properly prompted them to set up an early American village. The museum village, opened on a family farm site in 1950, was chartered as a nonprofit educational institution in 1961. It grew from several random buildings housing early tools into a complete village with extensive exhibits and personnel busy at old crafts. It has both original and reproduced 18th and 19th century buildings.

The age of homespun is portrayed in a log cabin in which such functions of everyday life as weaving, bootmaking, barbering and soap-making were performed in the 18th century. Cooking utensils and objects in everyday use are displayed on the first floor, while articles necessary for home weaving are arranged in a loft.

The village concentrates on the age of the craft shop; demonstrators take great pains not only to explain craft processes but to give you a thorough understanding of how their equipment works. The object of the shops that specialize in weaving, bootmaking, harness making and other industries is to indicate how a village cooperated during this period to make all needed objects. For example, the farmer took his flax to the weaving shop to be woven into cloth for him instead of his weaving it at home.

In the same way, the exhibits devoted to the age of industry illustrate how the nation, rather than the village, cooperated to become self-sufficient on a grand scale. In this age specialized factories began to supply products for all America. The cotton produced in the South could be man-ufactured into cloth in the East. The cloth could then be shipped to the North or West for manufacture into garments sold throughout the nation.

SMITHVILLE, NEW JERSEY

It could be said that a universal appetite for good food led to the success and expansion of the Smithville Inn, while at the same time an appetite and appreciation of Americana led to the creation by the inn's owners of the "historic towne of Smithville."

This museum village consists of 30 buildings, most of them moved to the site from points within New Jersey and reflecting life in early America. Shops and dwellings have been restored, an ancient grist mill grinds busily, and an early schooner is anchored in a three-acre man-made lake. Within the area of 2,500 acres, antiques and craft objects are displayed in such buildings as a buttery and a smoke house, while in others you may inspect early American furniture, pewter and brasses reproduced by master craftsmen.

"Possessors" of the village are Fred and Ethel Noyes Jr., who shared an enthusiasm for early

Plantation was re-created at Stone Mountain Park, Georgia

Americana. They were operators of an antiques shop in 1952, when they were smitten by the appearance of a long-vacant inn.

Mrs. Noyes describes the sequence of events in this way: *"Our story in reality commenced in 1787 when James Baremore, an itinerant New Englander, settled in Southern New Jersey and established the original Smithville Inn. He provided lodging for horses and man, for townspeople, and for stage coach travelers on the Long-A-Coming route.*

"The Inn reverberated with talk of politics, subjects of topical interest, and the like. It became the gathering place for drummers, tradepeople, every segment of society. Came the railroad through Central Jersey, the Inn suffered oblivion; the ravages of time and total neglect reduced the structure to a virtual shambles.

"My husband, Fred, and I passed by the old site, and a sight it was, on many of our foraging explorations through the area. At the time, we operated an antiques shop in nearby Absecon. We knew the beauty, the charm, the history reflected by the old, ramshackle Inn. We determined to 'possess' it, to restore an authentic landmark to the original social and economic status so long enjoyed, so soon forgotten.

"On May 1, 1952, our labor of love, now Historic Smithville Inn, reopened—two tiny rooms seating only 42 guests. We have added many rooms, many artifacts, many treasures since that day."

From the beginning, the inn was a success. It was enlarged a number of times and is today one of the village's three inns. Through the years, the couple refused to abandon their early preoccupation with antiques. They bought a general store, circa 1840, and moved it to their grounds. They stocked it with pot-bellied stove, a cracker barrel, and the usual advertising signs left behind by itinerant peddlers. They added a tobacconist shop, a red barn, a house, and a gradually increasing range of early American buildings.

The original dilapidated inn has become a township complex, employing close to 600 persons and still dependent for survival on hearty appetites for food and Americana.

STONE MOUNTAIN PARK, GEORGIA

This state park, 16 miles east of Atlanta, was conceived as a memorial to the contributions of the South to our American life and character. Perhaps best known among its variety of attractions is the famous carving on a gigantic scale of three major Confederate personalities, Pres-

ident Jefferson Davis, General Robert E. Lee and General Stonewall Jackson, depicted on horseback across the face of the mountain.

To be found in the 3000-acre recreational area around the base of the mountain are such tourist attractions as a Civil War Museum, an antique auto museum and a scenic railroad. But what sets a portion of the park apart as a museum village is a Deep South Plantation, its 18 buildings recalling the upper-class life of Georgia of more than a century ago.

The plantation is complete down to the smallest detail. Its staff tends flower gardens and crops, cures hams in the smokehouse and cares for farm animals in the barn. While the present staff is limited to a dozen or so, the plantation originally called for services by more than 75 persons.

The Big House was built in the 1840s as the plantation home of the Spring Creek Plantation at Dickey, Georgia. It was occupied by descendants until it was moved to Stone Mountain in 1961. The Kingston House, or overseer's house, was built around 1830 and reflects Greek Revival characteristics of the period. The house lay directly in the path of the rapidly advancing federal troops during their 1864 "march to the sea." It was, however, spared. Legend has it that General William Tecumseh Sherman used the home as headquarters for a brief period in May 1864. It was moved to Stone Mountain in 1962 from northwest Georgia.

As the plantation system developed in the South, plantations became small communities which were largely self-sufficient. Each had its own shops, warehouses, gardens and slave quarters. This is the kind of community represented here through buildings more than a century old.

WALNUT GROVE, SOUTH CAROLINA

The same community concept is achieved in an original setting at Walnut Grove Plantation, eight miles southeast of Spartanburg. The plantation originated with a grant from King George III in 1763 to Charles Moore, who built the manor house about 1765. The house remained in the family until 1961 when Mr. and Mrs. Tom Moore Craig deeded the property to the Spartanburg County Historical Association for restoration and administration. The Association has made the eight-acre tract an authentic interpretation of life in Spartanburg County prior to 1830.

The two-story frame dwelling is a Georgian-type structure with Queen Anne mantels, fielded pan-

Keeping room at Walnut Grove Plantation, Spartanburg, South Carolina

eling and double-shouldered chimneys. Out-buildings include a kitchen house, smoke house, drover's house and pump house. At the rear is located the Rocky Spring Academy, a classical school established by Charles Moore and operated from 1770 to about 1850. When school was not in session, it served as a weaving room.

In keeping with the plantation village concept, recent additions have been an 18th century log cabin and a wheat house, both moved from points within the state. Plans now call for reconstruction of a blacksmith shop and a doctor's office of the period.

LOREAUVILLE HERITAGE MUSEUM, LOUISIANA

More than 200 years ago French settlers in Canada's Acadia, now called Nova Scotia, were driven from their fertile lands. They settled in 1758 in southwestern Louisiana, where they prospered, spreading a French culture which in some degree survives today.

But through the years, much of the Acadian heritage and mode of life was lost. It was as a means of awakening local interest in the preservation of the culture, of Acadian past that a Loreauville native, Mrs. James Barras, launched her Loreauville Heritage Museum. To dramatize the need for preservation, Mrs. Barras sought to re-create an Acadian village, complete with authentic artifacts and accessories. She moved some buildings from their original sites and installed them on the museum grounds behind her home, near the banks of Bayou Teche. She equipped them with artifacts, tools, kitchen utensils and furniture.

The museum, through 32 units placed roughly in a rectangle, tells the story of the area from its colonial days to its life in the new Republic. It speaks of Indian life before the white man and of a simple trading post which later linked both.

Its exhibits span the homespun years of an Acadian village, connecting them with later industrial life.

GATLINBURG, TENNESSEE

Not all of life in the new Republic was peaches and cream in the early years or indeed late in the 19th century. This fact comes through in a number of museum villages, including Homespun Valley Mountaineer Village, a re-created community operated "as a tribute to the Old Timers, hardy mountaineers who until recent years were isolated deep within the high Smokies. By main strength, character, and the help of Providence they wrested a full life from the beautiful, crop-forbidding mountain sides."

The village, a major tourist attraction in Tennessee, is a working replica of the village of early mountaineer days, including hand looms, the cobbler shop, and Gatlinburg's first barber shop.

Here is the one-room log cabin once occupied by the Pink Hiskey family. The Caleb Trentham grist mill operated a century ago along Little Pigeon River nearby. Two museum buildings are crammed with memorabilia of local pioneers, including old glass, hog rifles, tools and clothes. A barn built about 1800 is a typical mountaineer two-stall barn constructed with logs, poles and hand-split shakes. Authentic to the early 19th century is a log school house, a still and outdoor stocks.

The village was started as a hobby by W. C. Postlewaite, publisher of *The Gatlinburg Press* and *The Sevier County News-Record*. It owes its present expanded status to contributions and the cooperation of other Gatlinburg residents. The aim throughout has been for authenticity. Buildings bought in other areas were photographed, their logs numbered on sketches, then dismantled piece by piece and reconstructed in the village.

Acadian Life is mirrored at Loreauville Heritage Museum, Louisiana

54

DEARBORN, MICHIGAN

Henry Ford, inventor of the Model T which revolutionized the auto industry, once said, "History is bunk, as it is taught in school." He believed that by looking at things people used and the way they lived a better and truer impression could be gained in an hour than could be had from a month of reading. He proved this to his satisfaction in 1929 by founding one of this country's greatest museums of American history, the Henry Ford Museum and Greenfield Village. It contains one of the most extensive collections of Americana in existence, tracing three centuries of American life and the development of its arts and skills.

The museum and the village are two separate entities, sharing the same grounds but telling the American story in different ways. The museum is a gargantuan edifice covering 14 acres. Henry Ford couldn't buy Philadelphia's Independence Hall, although he tried, so he had a replica built to serve as the museum entrance. To give that structure some distinguished company, he had Congress Hall and the old City Hall of Philadelphia duplicated adjacent to it, all three forming only a small part of the museum.

The museum's vast collection of Americana is arranged in three general sections. The development of American furniture and decoration is traced chronologically in the American Decorative Arts Galleries. Five blocks of late 18th and early 19th century shops preserve the tools and handiwork of pre-industrial industry along the Street of Early American Shops. Exhibits related to agriculture, industrial machinery, steam and electric power, communications, lighting and transportation are housed in Mechanical Arts Hall, which covers eight acres.

But it is on 260 acres adjoining that museum that historic buildings, transported from various parts of the country and restored, form Greenfield

Replica of Independence Hall is entrance of Henry Ford Museum

Thomas Edison's workshop at Greenfield Village

Village. All phases of American life are depicted in the nearly 100 structures.

Buildings that figured prominently in the political, social and religious life of the American community are grouped around the Village Green. These include the 1832 Clinton Inn, the first overnight stage stop on the route from Detroit to Chicago; the Martha-Mary Chapel of colonial-classic architecture, with its bell cast by the son of Paul Revere; and the Logan County Courthouse where young Abraham Lincoln practiced law while a circuit rider in frontier Illinois.

Craftsmen are busy daily in more than a dozen buildings which tell the story of American crafts and industries. The range of shops is as great as the range of their original locations. The Armington & Sims Machine Shop was operated in the 1880s and 1890s in Lawrence, Massachusetts. The Hanks Silk Mill was built in Mansfield, Connecticut, in 1810. The Plymouth Carding Mill was erected in Plymouth, Michigan, during the 1850s. Staves are formed in a cooper shop from Kingston, New Hampshire.

The homes of the village are outstanding examples of architecture and furnishings from three centuries of American living. They range from simple one-room log cabins, such as the birthplace of educator William Holmes McGuffey, to the elaborate home of Noah Webster, where his American dictionary was compiled. Other homes or birthplaces of famous Americans include those of the Wright Brothers, Henry Ford, Luther Burbank, Charles Steinmetz and Robert Frost.

As a tribute to his long-time friend, Henry Ford arranged a number of buildings tracing the career of Thomas A. Edison. These include a complex of buildings from Menlo Park, New Jersey, which formed the research center used by Edison from 1876 to 1886, and the Fort Myers, Florida, laboratory where Edison experimented with the production of rubber from American plants.

Special events enliven the village throughout the year. These range from an American Drama Festival, held during summer months, to a sports car review during the winter and a country fair of yesteryear in May.

56

Cotswold forge at Greenfield Village dates from early 1600s

5

The Westward Migration

EARLY in the 18th century the rugged Appalachian Mountains virtually sealed the seaboard colonies from territory to the West. Colonists, hungry for land of their own, heard enticing tales of the abundance of game and the fertility of the soil beyond the mountains, but the danger and rigors of a long journey over uncharted peaks, burdened by needed pack animals and supplies, were a strong deterrent to migration.

There were, of course, indirect routes to the West, and a number of the more daring took advantage of them. A favorite means of bypassing the mountains was by floating down rivers such as the Allegheny and the Monongahela to the Ohio River.

The migration west was made easier after 1750 when Dr. Thomas Walker, a Virginia physician and surveyor, discovered a natural passage through the mountain barrier. This was Cumberland Gap, today a national historic park.

Daniel Boone was hired by a land development company 25 years later to blaze a trail through the Gap to permit easy access by wagon. Boone, with the aid of 30 axmen, blazed a broad trail from Kingsport, Tennessee, into Kentucky.

At long last, new lands were made accessible through a route which posed comparatively few problems. The westward migration began and was given fresh impetus by the freedom gained by the Revolutionary War. For the daring there were new worlds to conquer and fortunes to be made in the rich lands to the west.

What the museum villages do in this new territory is to illustrate how virgin territory became homesite, farm and village for an expanding America.

BATH, OHIO

During its colonial days Connecticut claimed through royal grants a broad belt of land to its west, straight through Ohio. After the Revolutionary War, it bowed to pressure to free this interior territory by relinquishing its rights to all the interior land with the exception of a Western Reserve of nearly four million acres in northeastern Ohio.

In 1792 the state granted 500,000 acres to inhabitants of coastal towns whose property had been destroyed by British attack during the Revolution. It sold the rest of the land to speculators who urged New Englanders to move west to land they could buy for a dollar an acre. Ownership of land was a status symbol to colonists from Europe. The lure of inexpensive land was strong enough to

Early farmhouse at Western Reserve village, Bath, Ohio
Hale Homestead, 1825 dwelling of a pioneer

One-room schoolhouse in Burton, Ohio

bring more than 1300 settlers into the Western Reserve by 1800, many of them giving it a distinctively New England flavor.

Among later Connecticut settlers was Jonathan Hale, who in 1810 bought a farm in the Western Reserve. Hale's contribution to the growth of America was not as spectacular and colorful as the contribution of such figures as Daniel Boone, Andrew Jackson and Admiral Oliver Hazard Perry. But the contribution of Hale, and countless others like him, was an important one in taming the land and extending the sphere of civilized America. He prospered, took part in community affairs and in 1825 built a fine brick house.

The homestead remained in the family through generations until the 1960s when a great granddaughter, Miss Clara Belle Ritchie, bequeathed it to the Western Reserve Historical Society. It was her wish to have the house restored and operated as a museum which would mirror pioneer life. The society was delighted to follow her dictates. It restored the house and turned a barn at the rear into a museum of pioneer tools and crafts.

It then expanded its memorial to the reconstruction of a Western Reserve village, typifying

life between 1830 and 1840, on land across the road from the Hale Homestead. It moved to the site and restored a Connecticut salt-box, built in Richfield, Ohio, in 1830, and a Greek Revival house, erected in Bath, Ohio, 10 years later. The re-creation later continued with the addition of such structures as a law office, log cabin and schoolhouse, all around a village green.

Ohio's pride in the Western Reserve phase of its history is such that other museum villages on a similar scale were created. Pioneer Village in Canfield, Ohio, is a re-created settlement located within the Canfield Fairgrounds. While the grounds are open all year, tours of village buildings are made by appointment only.

The Western Reserve theme is repeated in Burton, Ohio, where the Geauga County Historical Society has moved a farmstead and other structures to a common site to portray rural life in the region in the 19th century. This museum village has, as its focal point the Eleazer Hickok home (1838) where period pieces are displayed. Other buildings with local historical significance are a country store, a primitive cabinet shop, school, church, barn and law office.

DEFIANCE, OHIO

Something different in the way of museum villages is Au Glaize Village, a 120-acre tract based on the belief that visitors like to join in doing things. The restoration project, begun in 1966 by the Defiance County Historical Society, is an attempt not only to recreate a village with buildings dating from 1860 to 1890, but also to provide a setting where the visitor becomes involved in the re-creation of history. He can help split shingles, chop logs for a building, skim sorghum molasses, or stir apple butter.

In the village are such structures as a church, railroad station, barbershop, school, sorghum mill, and tavern. A Black Swamp Farm on an 80-acre tract will eventually approximate a northwest Ohio farm of the early 19th century. There are nature trails throughout the village lands, all of which serve as a wildlife sanctuary.

MORGAN, OHIO

The museum village in Governor Bebb Park began with the donation of a single building to the Butler County Park District and ended with the reconstruction of an entire pioneer log village.

The building was the two-story log home with a one-story addition in which William Bebb, later governor of Ohio, was born on December 8, 1802. The original façade had been covered with new materials but the basic structure was sound when its owner, Carl Hesselbrock, offered the house to the Butler County Historical Society. A condition of the gift was its removal from the site in order that another dwelling might be built.

The society petitioned the park district to take over the house and in 1959 the district agreed. It bought a 10-acre site on a high bluff and moved the house by dismantling its 126 logs, some weighing more than 800 pounds. With this as a nucleus, the district launched a plan for a reconstructed pioneer village.

The original 10 acres of land were increased to 600. A cabin built in Indiana about 1850 and a split-rail fence joined the Bebb house. The village took shape with the addition of other log cabins and diverse structures, such as a covered bridge, once located outside of Oxford, Ohio.

Portion of pioneer log village in Morgan, Ohio

LITTLE ROCK, ARKANSAS

Arkansas, with its dense forests and rugged terrain, had little appeal to the early settlers. While some chose to make the territory their home in the late 18th century, it was not until 1803, when the United States took possession of Arkansas and the rest of the Louisiana Purchase lands, that the tide of migration rose.

Little Rock became the territorial capital in 1821, and it is here that the Arkansas Territorial Capitol Restoration provides a picture of Arkansas life of that time. The restoration in the heart of the city comprises a group of 13 original buildings on their original sites, occupying a half block of land. The nicely landscaped complex is enclosed by fences and set off by gardens.

One of the houses, built in 1820, served as the last meeting place of the Territorial Legislature in November, 1835. It was constructed of hand-hewn oak logs covered with cypress siding. In the upstairs Council Room, the wall boards have been left off to show the original log construction. Other buildings include the homes of Governor Elias N. Conway and of William E. Woodruff, founder of the *Arkansas Gazette* in 1819, oldest continuously published newspaper west of the Mississippi River.

The restoration is intended to recall the days of Arkansas' pre-statehood era, when pioneers were opening the new South and West. The restoration was made possible and financed in 1939 by the state.

Overall view of Arkansas Territorial Restoration, left.
Top, Territorial Capitol and, below, council chamber

Conner Home in Hamilton, Indiana

HAMILTON, INDIANA

The Conner Prairie Pioneer Settlement in Hamilton is a museum village which will tell you something about one of Indiana's foremost settlers and much about the early years of the state, when westward migration pushed further inland.

The settler was William Conner who, in 1800, became the first white man to set up a trading post along the White River. Conner prospered on trade with the Indians, served as a scout and interpreter for General William Henry Harrison and took part in the signing of many Indian treaties. Conner knew both the Indian and the white man's world intimately. He married the daughter of a Delaware chieftain soon after he established roots in the wilderness. In 1820 his wife chose to move westward with her six children when the Treaty of St. Mary's dictated that all Indians must migrate from the area. Conner, faced with the alternatives of joining the Indians or beginning a new life in the white community, chose the latter. Within a year he married Elizabeth Chapman and immersed himself in a life of business and politics. He lived a good, prosperous life,

served in the State Legislature and helped to found the cities of Noblesville and Alexandria.

Mainstay of the museum village is the two-story brick mansion which Conner built in 1823 as a home for Elizabeth. It so impressed a later philanthropist, Eli Lilly of Indianapolis, that he bought the house and property about it in 1930. He restored and refurnished the home and arranged for the restoration and reconstruction of other buildings of the period. Lilly presented the settlement to Earlham College in 1964 to be operated as a permanent historical museum.

The visitor today will learn, through the Conner home, something about the life of the wealthy and socially prominent during the 19th century. He will learn something about the luxuries of the period through outbuildings, such as the Still House where corn was processed into whiskey, the Spring House where cold, flowing water cooled perishable foods, and the Loom House where spinning and weaving produced cloth.

Conner's earlier life is depicted in three log structures, reconstructed to represent those in which he lived and worked with his Indian wife, Mekinges. These are a pioneer barn, housing a covered wagon and early implements; a trading post with goods used for barter with the Indians; and a pioneer cabin. Rounding out the village is a museum concentrated on frontier farming.

STONEFIELD, WISCONSIN

The museum village of Stonefield, located in Nelson Dewey State Park north of Cassville, tells the story of Wisconsin's agricultural beginnings. It centers around the plantation home of Nelson Dewey, first governor of the state. The home, built in the mid-19th century, is restored as an example of the home of a wealthy pioneer lawyer and farmer.

Visitors will get an inkling of early farm life in the estate's stone barns, which now house the State Farm Museum. They may then take a horse-drawn bus through a covered bridge to the streets of Stonefield Village, a life-size replica of a rural community of the 1890s.

These buildings, lining a village square and common to rural communities throughout the country, include a one-room school, general store and rural church. Shops represent those of the blacksmith, barber, banker and printer. Expansion of the village continues with the addition of early industrial buildings.

GRAND ISLAND, NEBRASKA

Nebraska, once regarded as a part of the "Great American Desert," was sold to the United States by Napoleon as a part of the Louisiana Purchase in 1803. Less glamorous than other western states which offered the prospect of a gold or silver strike, the territory did not feel the impact of westward migration until the latter half of the 19th century.

Pioneers heading for the fabled West rolled through Nebraska along the Oregon Trail. They failed to halt here in any great number until the Homestead Act of 1862 which enticed settlers to all parts of the West with its offer of 80- or 160-acre grants of land to those willing to develop them.

The Stuhr Museum of the Prairie Pioneer, aimed at making you see and feel the pioneer life of the plains between 1870 and 1915, was the outgrowth of a dream nurtured by members of the Hall County Historical Society since the 1920s, a dream to keep alive in some way the pioneer past of the region. In those early years members of the society, some of them pioneers themselves, collected relics and stored them in homes and barns. These implements, furnishings and other reminders of the past grew in number but con-

tinued to collect dust until Leo Stuhr, a farmer whose family settled in Grand Island in 1857, joined the preservation cause. In 1960 Stuhr donated to the society a tract of land as a museum site and $25,000 for construction of a museum building. Stuhr died a few years later and in his will bequeathed $550,000 to establish a museum dedicated to Nebraska's pioneer heritage.

The main museum building was designed by Edward Durell Stone of New York. He placed the square building on a circular man-made island in an artificial circular lake. In order to draw attention to the countryside as well as exhibits, he punctuated the building with strip windows. The windows provide natural light for exhibits arranged on two floors and views of the land to which the displays are related. The second-floor galleries have been set aside for exhibits which begin with the climate and the geographical background of the region, continue to exploration and settlement and close with the 1920s.

A large part of the 278 acres was set aside for the reconstruction of a turn-of-the-century farm, a small pioneer village, and a Pawnee Indian village.

Since its beginning in the summer of 1965, the pioneer village has progressed into a complex of more than 40 structures, including five houses, a bank building, railroad station, town hall and various business buildings. To give greater meaning to the village, the buildings are arranged according to a plan adopted by the Union Pacific Railroad for towns it once established along the railroad right of way. The plan calls for standard-width streets fronting on the railroad, which became the focal part of the town.

At Grand Island, most businesses front on a railroad siding where a small station, along with a collection of cars and a locomotive, are located. Buildings were acquired and moved from many points in Nebraska. The railroad station came from a town 75 miles to the west. Three barns and a blacksmith shop were moved from Aurora, 20 miles east. From other points came town houses, built between 1879 and 1890, including the Bell-Fonda cottage, furnished in the first decade of the 20th century and so named because actor Henry Fonda was born there in 1904.

In addition to the village proper, there is a log cabin complex, intended to be a teaching device. The unit is made up of cabins, a barn, smoke house and cook house.

At a distant point on the site a Danish Church built in 1888 stands tall, its shingled steeple

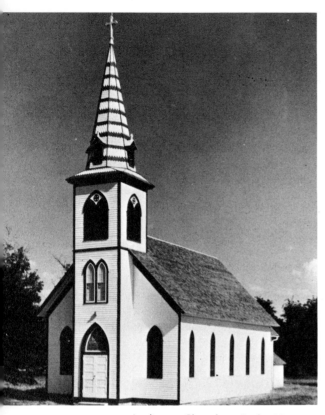

Lutheran Church at Stuhr Museum

Oconto railroad station at Stuhr

painted in a gay manner with green, white and gray stripes.

Waterways, including the Wood River, comprise an important part of the museum. Plans call for the re-creation along lakes, rivers and a canal of such structures as a missionary outpost, grist mill and Sioux encampment.

MINDEN, NEBRASKA

The Harold Warp Pioneer Village is designed to tell the story not only of the westward migration, but of America and how it grew. Like many other museum villages, it began in a small way, in this case with the acquisition of a rural school house. The school was offered for sale in 1948 and in time might have been demolished. It was rescued by Harold Warp, a native of Minden and a Chicago manufacturer who was determined the school he had attended as a child would not vanish from the American scene.

He later said, "With the country school house rapidly disappearing from the American scene, I determined to keep at least one of them intact. Then I decided to go ahead with my dream and

build a village—as a memorial to my parents and all of America's other pioneers—in which we would attempt to preserve one item of a kind of all the things the people used in settling and building our nation. With 1830 as a starting date, because that marks the start of mechanization, I wanted to show the evolution of all the marvels we enjoy today."

The village, clustered about a typical green, consists of 22 buildings on 20 acres. Warp and his assistants traveled hundreds of thousands of miles to locate and acquire suitable furnishings and relics. Their collection amounted to more than 30,000 items.

A modern museum building places its emphasis on the development of transportation, communications and entertainment. Transportation runs the gamut from horse-drawn vans to more than 200 antique autos and a replica of the Wright Brothers' history-making plane, the "Kitty Hawk."

Lesser buildings, authentic in their récreation or restoration, concentrate on the pioneer era. The Elm Creek Fort, a two-story log structure, was built in 1869 in Webster County, both as a dwelling

The Green is focal point at Pioneer Village at Minden, Nebraska

and as a community fort against Indian attack. The Bloomington Land office, originally located in Franklin County, once served pioneers filing their homestead claims. A sod house is a replica of the "little old sod shanty on the plain."

Some structures concentrate on a single facet of American life. The Fire House is a museum of fire-fighting equipment, while an agricultural building displays a collection of more than 500 agricultural implements in the order of their development.

BAKERSFIELD, CALIFORNIA

Kern County's Pioneer Village, located on 12 acres in the heart of Bakersfield, provides a broad panorama of frontier and later life in California. Through buildings and their exhibits, you may judge what was most important to sustain life in this region.

An exhibit of cattle branding irons attests to the importance of livestock to a growing economy. Horses were indispensable to the cattle industry, and as an acknowledgement of this the Roscoe Martin stock corral was moved from the

People's Store at Minden

site it occupied for a century to become a part of the village grounds. Later industry is represented by the oldest known operative cable-tool oil drilling rig, an exhibit of the 1910 period.

The Weller Ranch Ensemble includes a ranch house, hay derrick, windmill and other buildings. The house was built about 1890 in Rosedale by an Englishman brought to this country to aid in colonizing vast holdings of land barons.

The village has a cook wagon, used to feed the large crews of field hands employed by the Kern County Land Company in the 1880s, and the Alphonse Weill house (1882), first modern home in Bakersfield. The Bella Union Hotel, with its cafe, saloon and gambling hall, is typical of those throughout the West which catered to miners, loggers and cowboys in search of relaxation and a good meal.

Pioneer Village has these and many more—church, drug store, dentist's office, school and Chinese joss house—among its 30 buildings. A visit is a nostalgic journey into the vanished past of central California.

Sheepherder's cabin at Kern

Les girls entertain at Kern Pioneer Village

6

The Gold and Silver Rush

WITH THE DISCOVERY of America, the conviction was strong throughout Europe that this was a land rich in precious metals and gems. The conviction was fed by legends and rumors gained from Indians by early explorers of fabled cities built from solid gold and decorated with a vast array of gems.

The Spanish conquistadors found their gold in South America and plundered that continent to fill their nation's coffers. But the gold and silver of North America eluded the white man for several centuries. In their quest, thousands of the early explorers, principally Spanish, died in the rough and uncompromising wilderness that was America.

The precious metals were found from the mid-19th century on. Their discovery made many millionaires overnight. Tens of thousands of men were lured westward under the delusion that fortunes were easy to come by with the aid of a pick. Tracts of wilderness and mountainside were turned into boom towns overnight, swinging, two-fisted towns short of women and long on saloons and gambling devices. They began as a cluster of tents near an area where gold or silver had been mined and evolved into rows of rough wooden structures along streets which, with the least amount of rain, became seas of mud.

What set off the fortune-hunting stampede from East to West was the accidental discovery of gold in 1848 in the waters of a stream near Sutter's Fort in the valley of the Sacramento River. Gold fever struck the fledgling nation with great intensity. When President Polk affirmed that gold could be found in quantities which "would scarcely command belief," many an Eastern town was deserted by its younger men. Families sold their homes, packed their belongings in prairie wagons and began a 2000-mile journey West. Thousands left with hopes of great fortune, lost their dreams after privation, and ended up in unmarked graves along the way.

The migration, without parallel in the history of the world, blazed new trails to the Pacific. Some, such as the Oregon Trail, are still rutted by thousands of wagon wheels which etched the plains and deserts along the road West. The migration made a state of California and led to an exploration by prospectors of other territories in the West. Its impact was such that a number of states are now honeycombed with ghost towns, isolated and deteriorating groups of buildings which once pulsated with life.

Idaho, as an example, has 20 ghost towns in varying stages of disintegration. Its Department of Commerce and Development in Boise is happy to provide you with a list of them and a map. These include mud huts in Springtown, where Chinese miners lived while they panned gold.

Another, Moose City, once had a population of 9000 but can only be reached by horseback now. Silver City, in southwest Idaho, was once internationally famous when English companies developed its mines and uncovered a mass of solid ruby silver crystal weighing 500 pounds.

New Mexico, too, has a ghost town map, pinpointing communities which lived only while the veins of gold and silver remained rich. Some ghost towns, including one named Shakespeare, are run as museums with a charge for admission, while art studios and antique dealers are frequently the heart of others.

One of New Mexico's most famous ghost towns is Elizabethtown, northwest of Ute Park. For 30 years from 1866, it cut a wide swath in mining history and was renowned for its toughness and for its large population of Army deserters before it dwindled to a small number of persons who used a dredge to sift for gold in the Moreno district. The dredge, the "Eleanor," survived into the 1930s, when it disappeared into the mud.

Foremost among the states which have actively preserved mining towns as museum villages is California, where all the action began at Sutter's Mill. Most unusual of its mining museum villages is

BODIE STATE HISTORIC PARK, CALIFORNIA

You are advised, when you walk through old Bodie, to stay on the streets and sidewalks because most of the buildings are unsafe. They have been shored up and stabilized to preserve them. You are also warned to be wary of open mine shafts if you explore outside the area.

The town, with its brick and wooden buildings reminiscent of a Western movie set, was named after Waterman S. Bodie, who discovered gold nearby in 1859. Within 20 years Bodie had a population of more than 10,000. It also had a reputation for sin and lawlessness which gave it the distinction of possessing "the worst climate out of doors" and which inspired the frequently repeated witticism, "Goodbye, God, I'm going to Bodie." For relaxation after a hard day's work at the mines, the community had 65 saloons. The Reverend F. M. Warrington, during his brief pastoral service,

Miners once dreamed of fortunes in this Colorado ghost town

Stark buildings are reminders of lawless Bodie

described the town in 1881 as a "sea of sin, lashed by the tempests of lust and passion."

Another view was presented in the book *The Saga of Wells Fargo* in this way: "*At the high noon of its great days there were 30 mines in operation in Bodie . . . and the saloons, pothouses, restaurants, gin mills, ale stoops and allied and adjacent deadfalls averaged, according to the advertising columns in the Bodie Standard, something better than one to a mineshaft. Having dined at Stewarts Hotel, the Arlington, the Bodie House, Brown's or . . . the Occidental, Grand, Central or Windsor, the workman off duty was confronted by a bewildering choice of oases on which to lavish his patronage.*

"*He had his choice of Wagner's Corner, the Parole Saloon, the Rifle Club, the Cabinet, the Senate, the Commercial, the Champion, Peters and Aldriges, the Gymnasium, Mark's Saloon, the Sawdust Corner or the Bonanza. At all of these, the products of the town's three breweries—the Bodie, the Pioneer, the Pat Fahey's—were the favored chasers.*

"*. . . There was almost sure to be a company of East Lynn or Ten Nights in a Bar Room, both prime favorites, performing at the Miners' Union Hall. And, after the show, at an hour when life was really in order, the prudent reveler could save his final and best thirst of the evening to be dissipated at one or both of the town's ranking resorts of quality and fashion: the Maison Doree Restaurant, where the best quail in aspic in all the Esmeralda region was served for supper, or the Philadelphia Beer Depot, opposite to Wells Fargo, the handsomest saloon in Bodie and patronized by all classes—sandwiches for customers at all hours. The river of life flowed at its fullest in Bodie, both around and through its citizens.*"

Bodie, designated a state historic park in 1962 and maintained in a state of "arrested decay," may be inspected on a walking tour. The state has established 32 posts along the walk, pointing out the more unusual points of interest. A nicely written state leaflet provides nuggets of information. It states that a small sawmill used for cutting firewood was essential to cope with winters during which temperatures dropped to 40 degrees below zero and snow accumulated to heights of 20 feet. On Maiden Lane and Virgin Alley resided many of the town's "ladies," such as The Beautiful Doll, Madame Mustache and Rosa May.

Visible on the nearby slope of Bodie Bluff is the Standard Mine and Mill, which yielded nearly $15 million in gold during 25 years. This and other mines at Bodie produced bullion estimated at more than $90 million.

The Bodie store and warehouse, or Boone's Store, has siding and roofing partially formed with the metal from five-gallon cans. The cans originally contained kerosene and gasoline, hauled in from Hawthorne and Carson City.

Apart from houses, shops and streets which once resounded with vigorous life, you may inspect four fenced-in cemeteries used for burial of respectable citizens and, outside the fenced-in areas, a "Boot Hill" where the lawless were laid to rest, in most cases without markers.

BARSTOW, CALIFORNIA

Calico Ghost Town, once Southern California's greatest silver camp, owes its existence to the preservation efforts of Walter Knott, descendant of a pioneer family and a prominent businessman. Knott bought the town and restored it as a salute to those who lived and worked in Calico during its mining heyday. He deeded the village in 1966 to the County of San Bernardino for operation as a regional park.

Knott had a personal interest in Calico. His uncle, John C. King, sheriff of San Bernardino County from 1879 to 1882, grubstaked two prospectors who discovered the richest Calico deposits. Knott himself worked as a young man in the Calico mines for a summer.

Within a few years of the silver strike in 1881, more than 3000 persons inhabited the growing community, building and staffing such establishments as Lil's Saloon, Lane's Mercantile Store, the Maggie Mine Commissary and Lucky Joe's Palace. As the price of silver rose, the town prospered. Within 15 years the mines had produced more than $86 million in high-grade silver ore. The boom "busted" in 1896 when the silver veins began to play out and the price of silver dropped. The sands of the desert sifted in to obliterate streets and buildings deserted by men and women who trekked to greener pastures.

Today, hundreds of shafts and tunnels in the Calico Mountains are silent reminders of mines which operated around the clock. The restoration of the town to its appearance in the 1880s is concentrated along Main Street, lined by buildings erected in their original haphazard pattern. Here once again stand the assay shop, the pottery works, confectionary store and fire house. A collection of paintings, "Gunslingers of the Old West," by Lea Franklin McCarty hangs in Lil's Saloon. Existing ruins of structures are being carefully preserved, while many buildings which vanished with time have been recreated.

BUENA PARK, CALIFORNIA

Walter Knott, a restaurateur who ran the profits from a boysenberry road stand into a multi-million dollar food and recreation business, has also created his own Ghost Town, with many commercial touches, at Knott's Berry Farm, Buena Park. The Knott enterprises, built on a 200-acre site, embrace Americana as well as food and entertainment. Knott imported period buildings and reconstructed others as a tribute to the ways and the people of the Old West. Along the streets with old boardwalks set with polished squarehead nails, you'll find such buildings as the Wells Fargo Office, Silver Dollar Saloon, Chinese laundry, blacksmith shop and livery stable.

COLUMBIA STATE HISTORIC PARK, CALIFORNIA

Like Bodie, the gold rush town of Columbia is preserved and operated by the state. This "gem of the southern mines" was one of more than 500 mining towns that sprang up in the Gold Belt in.

Schoolhouse at Calico

The store is gathering place at Knott's Ghost Town

Restored Columbia lives on in California's gold country

the 1840s and 1850s. More than half that number today are little more than historic ruins.

Unlike Bodie, Columbia never reached the ghost town status. Although its population dwindled after 1860, when easily mined placer gold was exhausted, it retained its status as a community and much of its original appearance through the years. It remained a town until 1945, when the state created Columbia State Historic Park as a means of preserving a typical gold rush town.

Columbia sprang to life in March 1850 with a gold strike which within a month attracted more than 5000 prospectors to the area. The first tents and shanties gave way to permanent structures. Within two years the town had more than 150 places of business, including 30 saloons and a brewery. And within 10 years more than $87 million in gold was taken from its mines.

In common with other mining towns in the West, this one had its Chinese quarter, made up of immigrants brought into the country under contract to work the mines. Most remained in the United States to prospect on their own or to operate their own businesses.

The Chinese influence lingers on today in such shops as laundries and restaurants. The town also testifies to the serious attempts to bring culture into the community, in the Fallon Theater, built in the late 1880s, and to the early desire for education in a school house built in 1860 and used for classes as late as 1937.

The State has restored the Wells Fargo office, the brick school house with its bell tower and pot-bellied stoves and other significant buildings. It has also opened a number of period stores and shops.

ALDER GULCH, MONTANA

California, of course, had no corner on gold. One of many important gold discoveries in the West was made in May 1863, when six men found rich placer ground in Alder Gulch, then a part of Idaho Territory and now a part of Montana. The gulch quickly became an 18-mile-long mining camp. Two communities in the gulch, Virginia City and Nevada City, today are not museum villages in the strictest sense. However, they retain and preserve enough of the original mining camp flavor to warm the heart of any Old West buff. Old buildings have been restored and stocked as they were in the 1860s and 1870s, and some are maintained as historical museums.

It is estimated that $100 million was panned and dug from Alder Gulch through the years but, as in other gold mining communities, the pickings became slimmer and slimmer. Mining camps were deserted and Nevada City became a ghost town by the close of the 19th century. Only Virginia City survived as a working and mining community.

In 1946 a restoration program was launched to re-create the early mining town atmosphere of Nevada City. This has been done by the Virginia City Trading Company, which has furnished structures and turned them into museums, using income derived from commercial enterprises.

Virginia City, on the other hand, has buildings dating from the 1880s which still house offices and shops. Both communities have set up tourist accommodations, their façades resembling shacks and structures of the gold rush days.

In its heyday, the gulch attracted the lawless who hoped to gain with the gun what others were gaining by sweat and luck. There were 190 murders within a seven-month period, leading to the formation of a Vigilante Committee which assiduously hunted down more than a score of road agents. Contributing to the rule of the gun was "Robber's Roost" 12 miles from Virginia City, de-

scribed in a highway sign in the following manner:

"In 1863 Pete Daly built a road house on the stage route between Virginia City and Bannack to provide entertainment for man and beast. The main floor was a shrine to Bacchus and Lady Luck. The second floor was dedicated to Terpsichore, and bullet holes in the logs attest the fervor of ardent swains for fickle sirens. Occasionally a gent succumbed.

"Pete's Tavern became a hangout for unwholesome characters who held up stage coaches and robbed lone travelers. One of the road agents is alleged to have left a small fortune in gold cached in the vicinity.

"In later years, time and neglect gave the building its present hapless look, and it became known as Robber's Roost. It is in the cottonwood grove just across the railroad tracks. Drive over and pay your respects, but please don't dig up the premises trying to locate the cache."

If you are concerned about technical matters, Virginia City is a place where you may learn about the various methods of mining. Placer gold, which first made Alder Gulch famous, is washed by weather from rock into streams or pockets. This was gold which could be had for the taking with-

The saloon once packed them in at Virginia City, Montana

Robber's Roost,
above, near
Virginia City,
Montana, was
hangout for
hold-up gangs.
At left,
soda fountain
was part of store
in Nevada City,
sister mining
camp to Virginia
City, Nevada

Railroad still runs between Nevada City and Virginia City, two restored mining towns. Below, first church still stands in Bannack, a booming mining town in the 1860s

out great labor. Gold could be sifted and sorted by means of a gold pan or a sluice box. When the supply of placer gold diminished, companies resorted to quartz or hard-rock mining to free the precious metal from other elements in which it was held. Having built tunnels and shafts into the ground, men carted the gold-veined earth into crushing and smelting plants where the gold was separated from the dross. In the 1890s, dredge boats were hauled in to scoop the earth out of creeks, bars and banks and to separate nuggets from dirt and rock. In 1915 dredging operations

brought in $800,000 from six million cubic yards of gravel. Dredging operations continued into the 1940s. Even today a number of enterprising individuals are making plans to locate and refine the gold that exists in Alder Gulch.

SOUTH PASS CITY, WYOMING

Wyoming, best known today for its cattle and oil lands, once had its shining moment in the golden sun. It was the mecca of tens of thousands of prospectors who established towns which had a brief life span.

South Pass City in Wyoming sprawled on the Oregon Trail

In memory of those pioneering years, Wyoming State Archives Department in Cheyenne has prepared a map pinpointing the location of 53 ghost towns, most notable among which is South Pass City, a town born with the discovery of a rich lode of gold in June 1867. Within a year South Pass City had a Main Street a half mile long, crowded with shops, hotels and saloons. Its population jumped to 2000, then receded as the gold deposits played out. Within a decade the town was finished, well on its way to its eventual ghost town status.

But during its brief moment in history, South Pass City made a number of contributions to the direction of the country. One of its residents, William H. Bright, was author of a bill giving equal suffrage to women. The town was a county seat and site of the first Masonic lodge in Wyoming.

The town was desolate and decayed when the state's 75th Anniversary Commission bought it in 1964 with the idea of restoring it. The commission has since turned it into a colorful museum village through restoration and recreation of its principal buildings.

7

Lincoln and the Civil War

OF ALL THE WARS in America's history, none was as gallant and chivalrous and at the same time more tragic than the Civil War, which saw brother fighting against brother and neighbor against neighbor. And perhaps of all our wars, none produced so heroic and unexpected a national leader as Abraham Lincoln.

The federal government, like an old soldier responding to the distant sound of taps, has saluted the warriors of both sides by setting aside as national monuments large areas which once were arenas of battle. To a lesser degree, states and cities have followed suit, providing an impressive documentation of just how it was during the thunder of the 1860s.

The government's far-ranging salute extends into many states, representing a roll call of good men and true who fell on both sides. Among sites under federal jurisdiction are those which comprise such significant chapters of history as the following.

In South Carolina, Fort Sumter National Monument was the island bastion in Charleston Harbor which became the target of the first shots fired by Confederate forces. The assault on April 12, 1861, less than four months after South Carolina seceded from the Union, led to abandonment of the fort by Federal troops.

In Tennessee, Shiloh National Military Park commemorates one of the fiercest military engagements in history, in which during two April days in 1862 more than 23,000 men fell in battle.

Pennsylvania's Gettysburg National Military Park, immortalized by Lincoln's classic address, is remembered as the site of the most decisive battle of the Civil War, the springboard from which General Robert E. Lee hoped in 1863 to launch his great invasion of the North.

These and dozens of other areas set aside as monuments to the War Between the States have been studied and re-examined by history buffs through the years. So have many of the Lincoln shrines, restorations and re-creations along a broad swath of states which are a part of the Lincoln Heritage Trail.

Museum villages which are open to you include one in which the thunderclouds of war gathered and another in which peace was proclaimed.

HARPERS FERRY, WEST VIRGINIA

Many acts of hostility and violence preceded the secession of the Southern states and the formation of the Confederacy. The basic issue of slavery versus emancipation inflamed the passion of the nation and produced scores of partisans willing to die for their cause.

One such partisan was John Brown, a Connecticut native, New York State resident and militant abolitionist leader. It was Brown's dream to free groups of slaves, by force if necessary, and to equip them as part of his army. He envisioned the day when he could aid them in setting up totally free communities somewhere on the vast lands of America. Brown had his own band of visionaries, ready to battle for the cause at his command. Battle the small army did at a sleepy village called Harpers Ferry.

The site was little more than a small group of cabins when Robert Harper in 1747 bought land in the shadow of the Blue Ridge Mountains where the Shenandoah and Potomac Rivers meet and established a ferry service. With water power at hand, he built a mill and watched with satisfaction as a village grew about his enterprises. Some years later, President George Washington persuaded Congress that Harpers Ferry was "the most eligible spot on the river" for a federal armory. Raw materials, such as iron and hardwood, were on hand for the manufacture of arms, and ships could

quickly bring these arms by way of the Potomac to the seacoast. In subsequent years, rifles by the thousands were made and stored at Harpers Ferry. It was this abundance of arms that John Brown sought to seize in 1859.

Brown organized his fatal expedition with great care. He arrived at Harpers Ferry on July 3, 1859, masquerading as a land and cattle buyer with the name of Isaac Smith. He rented the Kennedy farm five miles north of town and during the summer months drilled his small contingent of troops, including two of his sons.

At last ready for his grand move, Brown led a party of 18 men into the town on Sunday night, October 16. Total success was theirs—at first. They captured the armory watchman and turned the fire engine house of the armory into a barricade. They collected hostages and slaves and, convinced the town was theirs, waited for the dawn. Daylight, however, brought with it the beginning of disaster. Townspeople fired at the engine house and posted themselves at the Shenandoah Bridge, one of their escape routes. Militia from nearby

John Brown made history here at Harpers Ferry

Charles Town poured in, taking up positions along the Potomac Bridge and cutting off another avenue of escape. Firing continued throughout the day, with the preponderance of fire growing heavily on the part of the townspeople. Innocent bystanders and town residents were casualties. Both of Brown's sons were fatally wounded. The odds were heavily against Brown with the arrival on Monday night of Colonel Robert E. Lee and Lieutenant J.E.B. Stuart with ninety Marines. The Marines battered in the door of the building and entered with slashing bayonets. The dead numbered 10 on Brown's side, four townspeople, and one Marine.

Brown was brought to trial in Charles Town, pleading innocence of everything but "a design on my part to free slaves." He was hanged on December 2, providing abolitionists in the North with a martyr and fresh cause for renewed militancy.

For Harpers Ferry a tranquil life was for many years only a long memory. The arms which had brought it prosperity now brought it repeated woe. At the outset of the Civil War in April 1861,

Virginia militia mounted an assault on the community, hoping to capture its stock of weapons. Federal troops retaliated by putting the torch to the arsenal, destroying more than 15,000 rifles.

Time and again its location made Harpers Ferry a pawn in the war. It was occupied by Union forces and infiltrated by Confederate troops, who burned the flour mill. It was caught between the opposing armies in 1862 and 1863, losing a building here and another there during hostilities. For the next two years it served the Union as a supply base for General Philip Sheridan's campaign through the Shenandoah Valley.

At war's end, Harpers Ferry was virtually a ghost town. In a sense, it continues to be one today. As a national historic park, it recalls the ghosts of those Civil War years when great men and great events conspired to destroy it. No longer standing are the arsenals or the fire engine house in which John Brown made his stand. But the remaining buildings, numbering more than two score and including a John Brown Museum, rest solidly along silent streets, like daguerreotypes holding for all of time something of the long past.

General Lee surrendered here at Appomattox Court House

APPOMATTOX COURT HOUSE, VIRGINIA

Virginia, capital of the Confederacy, was the site of more than half the fighting in the Civil War. Much of the military strategy was planned and directed by a native son, Robert E. Lee, whose birthplace is now a historic shrine and a working plantation.

Appropriately, it was in the Virginia village of Appomattox Court House, now a national historic park, that the Civil War came to an end on April 9, 1865. It was here in the McLean house that General Ulysses S. Grant and General Lee met to draft surrender terms. It was here, with the war officially over, that Confederate troops stacked their arms and left for home.

Union General Joshua L. Chamberlain described the meeting between Grant and Lee in this way: *"There behind me, riding in between my two lines, appeared a commanding figure, superbly mounted, richly accoutred, of imposing bearing, noble countenance, with expression of deep sadness overmastered by deeper strength. It is no other than Robert E. Lee!*

"Not long after, by another inleading road, appeared another form, plain, unassuming, simple, and familiar to our eyes, but to the thought as much inspiring awe as Lee in his splendor and his sadness. It is Grant!

"Slouched hat without cord; common soldier's blouse, unbuttoned, on which, however, the four stars; high boots, mud-splashed to the top; trousers tucked inside; no sword, but the sword-hand deep in the pocket; sitting his saddle with the ease of a born master, taking no notice of anything, all his faculties gathered into intense thought and mighty calm. He seemed greater than I had ever seen him."

Union General George A. Forsyth, writing of the meeting, described the town as a "courthouse, a small tavern, and eight or ten houses, all situated on this same road or street." General Grant and staff, he went on, "rode to Mr. McLean's house, a plain two-story brick residence in the village, to which General Lee had already repaired, and where he was known to be awaiting General Grant's arrival.

"Dismounting at the gate, the whole party crossed the yard, and the senior officers present went up on to the porch which protected the front of the house. It extended nearly across the entire house and was railed in, except where five or six steps led up to the centre opposite the front door, which was flanked by two small wooden benches, placed close against the house on either side of the entrance.

"The door opened into a hall that ran the entire length of the house, and on either side of it was a single room with a window in each end of it, and two doors, one at the front and one at the rear of each of the rooms, opening on the hall. The room to the left, as you entered, was the parlor, and it was in this room that General Lee was awaiting General Grant's arrival."

At about four o'clock the conference ended and with it the war ended. The McLean house and other structures in the village have been restored and furnished. They are now part of a one-and-a-half-square-mile park.

THE LINCOLN HERITAGE TRAIL

A 2500-mile network of highways mapped by the states of Illinois, Indiana and Kentucky in 1962 as a suggested motor itinerary for tourists, the Trail follows the footsteps of Lincoln from his birth near Hodgenville, Kentucky, to his burial in Springfield, Illinois. At the same time, it exposes the motorist to state parks and attractions along the way.

The Lincoln story as told by museums and historic sites along the trail begins with the migration of the President's grandfather, also named Abraham Lincoln, from the Shenandoah Valley of Virginia into Kentucky in 1780. Markers indicate where the family, which included five children, settled on the Green River Lick. Abraham was slain by Indians in 1786, and his widow Bathsheba moved to Washington County to a new farm in the wilderness. A portion of that farm, five miles north of Springfield, Kentucky, is now the Lincoln Homestead State Shrine. Here is found the Lincoln Cabin, a replica of the log house in which Bathsheba raised her children. Furnished in pioneer style, it rests on the same spot as the original cabin.

Close by is a blacksmith shop, a reproduction of the building in which her son Thomas learned his woodworking trade. The shop now houses tools and materials of the Lincoln era. Thomas' teachers in this shop were Richard and Francis Berry, both master craftsmen. It was inevitable under this arrangement that Thomas should meet Nancy Hanks, niece of Richard Berry, in whose home she resided. That home, moved from the Beechland section about a mile away, is the third building in the complex. In the living room of the restored structure before the immense fireplace Tom proposed to Nancy. On display here are pioneer relics and photostatic copies of the marriage bonds of the President's parents.

In 1803, Thomas Lincoln acquired a farm on Mill Creek in Harden County, Kentucky. This is where the Abraham Lincoln story really begins. Lincoln wrote in his autobiography, *"I was born Feb. 12, 1809 in then Hardin county, Kentucky, at a point within the now recently formed county of Larue, a mile, or a mile and a half from where Hodginsville now is."*

Ten years after their marriage, the Thomas Lincolns moved to what they hoped would be more fertile pastures in southern Indiana. These were to be Abe Lincoln's formative years, from the age of seven. He later wrote, *"I can remember our life in Kentucky; the cabin, the stinted living, the sale of our possessions, and the journey with my father and mother to Southern Indiana. We removed to what is now Spencer County, Indiana, in the autumn of 1816, I then being in my eighth year. This removal was partly on account of slavery, but chiefly on account of the difficulty in land titles in Kentucky."*

Abe helped with construction of the pioneer cabin in an area of wooded hills and forests. He wept at the death of his mother two years later and gained a friend and counselor a year later in his stepmother, the widow Sarah Bush Johnston. He went to school "by littles," cleared the land, and split fence rails. He borrowed books by the score and read them by the light of the fireplace. A memorial which brings to life the spirit of these important years in Lincoln's life, is located in Rockport, Indiana.

LINCOLN PIONEER VILLAGE

This museum village, designed by George Honig, artist and sculptor, is intended to represent the life and times of Lincoln and his pioneer neighbors during the 14 years he spent in Spencer County. It consists of more than a dozen buildings, some of them restored and others replicas, which picture life of the period.

Facets of Lincoln's life come through in such reproduced structures as John Pitcher's law office, where Abe borrowed many a book and carried it to his home seventeen miles away, the Jones store in which Lincoln was briefly employed as a clerk and a pioneer schoolhouse much like the one Lincoln attended.

A number of buildings are sponsored by individuals and by organizations. The Gentry mansion

Lincoln cabins in Lincoln Homestead State Park in Kentucky

is sponsored by descendants of James Gentry, a neighbor of the Lincolns, who hired Lincoln in 1828 to go with his son Allen on a flatboat to New Orleans. The home of Azel Dorsey, one of Abe's schoolteachers, is sponsored by the Rockport Garden Club. The floor is made of puncheons, heavy pieces of roughly dressed timber, hewed with a broad ax and put down with pegs.

Old Pigeon Baptist Church is a replica of the structure which Thomas Lincoln and his son Abe helped to build. Another replica is the Lincoln homestead in Spencer County, its stairway of pegs driven into the wall leading to a loft similar to the one in which Abe made his bed.

In March 1830 Thomas Lincoln again sought new horizons and turned to Illinois, the state in which Abraham Lincoln was to achieve greatness. The family settled briefly in Decatur, where their farm is now a part of a state park. In the summer, Thomas Lincoln moved his family to a new farm in Coles County, while Abraham Lincoln set out to carve his own life in New Salem.

NEW SALEM STATE PARK, ILLINOIS

It was in New Salem that Abe found himself. During his six years in this village of about a hundred persons he worked as a store clerk, postmaster, mill hand and surveyor. He studied law by the light of burning shavings in the fireplace of Henry Onstott's cooperage. He drilled with other militia volunteers before leaving to fight in the Black Hawk War, in which he served as captain. He gained such respect that he was elected to the Illinois General Assembly in 1834.

During Lincoln's life in New Salem, the town grew rapidly in size and stature. Two years after he left for New Springfield the county seat was established at Petersburg, and New Salem withered rapidly.

In 1906 the town appeared to be headed for extinction when William Randolph Hearst bought the historic town and transferred it in trust to the Chautauqua Association. The site was turned over to the state in 1916 and in the following year became a state park. Through the years, the town has been reconstructed building by building. The one original building is the Onstott Cooper shop, moved from its original New Salem location to Petersburg in 1840 and returned to its original site in 1922. The buildings have been re-created and furnished in such a manner that the park today is a most impressive memorial.

Abe's early life is reflected at Lincoln Pioneer Village, Indiana

Statue depicts young Lincoln in New Salem, Illinois

Reproduced village of New Salem, where Lincoln spent six years .

Trees, flowers and vegetable gardens were planted for historical authenticity. Furnishings include many articles used in New Salem during Lincoln's day.

The buildings are old friends to students of Lincoln lore. The Rutledge Tavern was home to Lincoln during a period when he slept in its loft. Legend has it that he courted Ann Rutledge, daughter of the innkeeper, until her death by fever. Weeping at her grave, he said, "My heart is buried there."

The Berry-Lincoln Store is one of two which Lincoln owned in partnership with William F. Berry. In the Miller and Kelso Cabin Lincoln frequently discussed Shakespeare and other classics of literature. In the Hill-McNamar Store he probably served a portion of his postmastership. These were Abe Lincoln's flowering years, the years of his lesser triumphs. His major accomplishments, and his major burden, came after his move, in 1837, to Springfield to practice law and engage in politics.

Springfield, Illinois, the end of the Lincoln Heritage Trail, has a number of buildings which trace the story of his marriage, his election to Congress and his role as President. In the Edwards Home, built in 1836, Abe courted, proposed to, and in 1842 married Mary Todd of Lexington, Kentucky, the sister of Mrs. Ninian Edwards. Following Lincoln's assassination Mrs. Lincoln retreated to this house, where she remained until her death.

The Lincoln home nearby, the only one he ever owned, is a plain building in which three of his children were born and from which he departed for Washington to assume the presidency. Across the street is the Abraham Lincoln Museum with its documents of the Civil War period and its dioramas depicting Lincoln's life.

At Oak Ridge Cemetery is the impressive Lincoln Tomb and Monument, final resting place not only for Lincoln but for his wife and three of their four sons. It is this monument, along with others on the historic trail, that perpetuates the life and the legend of Abraham Lincoln.

8

The Wild West

THE WILD WILD WEST was wild indeed, due in large measure to the cowboy who played a major role in its development. The cowboy, through the pen of Bret Harte, Owen Wister and other writers, became and remains a distinctly American folk hero, molded in the image of a laconic, leathery, hard-riding, trigger-tempered range rider.

He came into prominence in the decades immediately after the Civil War when Americans by the thousands migrated to the promising lands of the West. At about the same time, businessmen weighed the potential of the new territory and began construction of a cross-country railroad. As the rails inched westward, the cattle industry boomed. It was now possible to drive cattle from lush range land to a railroad terminus, capitalizing on the demand from the East for fresh beef.

In your exploration of the West, you will find scores of museums and building complexes touching on the history of the West and its famous and infamous personalities. You will also find some groups of buildings intended to re-create the spirit, if not the fact, of the wild West.

An example is the combined re-creation and restoration of Medora, North Dakota, made famous by Theodore Roosevelt, who ranched near the town in the 1880s before he became President.

Situated in the Bad Lands, at the entrance of Theodore Roosevelt National Memorial Park, Medora was founded in 1883 by the French nobleman, the Marquis de Mores, who envisioned the town as the center of a cattle and meat packing empire. Within three years, the Marquis' venture proved a financial catastrophe. Within seven years Medora was little more than a ghost town.

The town was acquired in the early 1960s by a history buff, Harold Schafer, on behalf of the Gold Seal Company which he headed. The company has since restored major buildings in Medora and put them to use. Its goal has been to capture the spirit of the Wild West as Roosevelt knew it and to place the town on a self-sustaining basis as a tourist attraction.

Rooms in the Rough Riders Hotel and above the Joe Ferris General Store, where Roosevelt maintained living quarters when he came to town, were furnished authentically and are now guest facilities. The company has also restored the 26-room chateau of the Marquis de Mores and the ranch home of Teddy Roosevelt. It made available horses for hire and built a new motel nearby.

Purely for the tourist is Old Tucson, movie location and studio located 12 miles west of downtown Tucson, Arizona. The town was built by

Ranching home of Theodore Roosevelt in Medora, North Dakota

Rough Riders Hotel, Medora

Chateau, Medora

Columbia Studios in 1939 as a replica of early Tucson and has since been used as the setting for scores of films and television shows. Visitors are free to stroll through Mexican Plaza with its water fountain, early cantina, and ancient adobe buildings. They may also visit an Apache Indian village and a typical ranch house. To add authenticity to Old Tucson, its employees dress in western costume of the early period and streets echo with gunshots during daily re-enactments of Old West episodes.

But, for the feel of a town which lived up to the reputation of the Wild West, journey to

TOMBSTONE, ARIZONA

With gold and silver strikes long an established fact in the West, prospector Ed Schieffelin risked death at the hands of hostile Apaches by searching the San Pedro hills of Arizona for silver. He shrugged off a warning by soldiers at Fort Huachuca that all he would find was his tombstone.

Schieffelin found his silver mine in September 1877. Recalling the warning given him when he set out for the forbidding region of mountain and desert, he named his claim "the Tombstone." It was logical that the fast-growing mining camp nearby should assume the same designation.

Three years later the town's newspaper, the *Epitaph,* got its name after founder-editor John Clum reasoned that *"every Tombstone needs its Epitaph."*

Before Schieffelin was through prospecting he had staked out four mining areas in the Loma de

Plata, or Hill of Silver. Hordes of other prospectors and miners who moved in on news of his good fortune located and claimed others.

Within four years, booming Tombstone was the seat of the newly formed Cochise County, with a population of more than 12,000 persons. It was also a mecca for cowboys, gunmen and fortune hunters, seeking by hook or crook to make their own a portion of the more than $25 million dug from the mines. For the decade that Tombstone boomed, the main thoroughfare of Allen Street had saloons and gambling halls open day and night. The misfortunes which befell some of the lawless were such that Boot Hill Cemetery, located on the outskirts of the town with a fine view of mountains and desert, grew to 180 graves.

Today, you will find mesquite bushes growing between the rows of white crosses, on which simple inscriptions tell their laconic tales—*"Shot by a Chinaman," "Hanged by Mistake,"* or *"Killed in a Gunfight."*

Shootings there were by the dozens, but none so much a part of Western legend as the Battle of the O.K. Corral, which took place on October 27, 1881, during the brief tenure as city marshal of Virgil Earp. The famous Earp brothers were noted in the West for their proficiency with the six-gun and their willingness to use it. Through the years they made enemies, among them the brothers Ike and Billy Clanton, both reputedly quick on the draw.

Out of this classic situation came the classic shoot-out. Marshal Earp and his brothers, Morgan and Wyatt, along with their ailing friend, Doc Holliday, were in Tombstone. Outside the town and spoiling to even the score with the Earps were the Clantons with three cowpuncher friends, the brothers Tom and Frank McLowery and Billy Clairborne. The Clanton group of five rode into town, gathering at the corral on Fremont Street. In the early afternoon, the three Earp brothers, accompanied by Doc Holliday, headed there, guns on their hips. The streets cleared, guns blazed, and the results were counted. Frank and Tom McLowery were dead. Billy Clanton suffered a fatal wound. Virgil and Morgan Earp were grazed by bullets.

Tombstone today calls itself "the town too tough to die." In the 12 years it flourished, fires gutted its main buildings and the shafts of its silver mines filled with water, slowing and then halting operations. By 1890 nearly all mining activity had ceased. Historic buildings began to disintegrate as the population dwindled.

Tombstone, however, never became a ghost town. Its inhabitants, numbering in the hundreds, found other means of livelihood. In 1925 individuals and organizations beyond the town limits began to restore a few buildings, aiming for the tourist market. Concern for the old town was sharpened in 1964 when new funds, these from the East, were made available to restore and re-create buildings of the town's heyday. Schieffelin Hall, an august theater built in 1881, was restored. The Crystal Palace Saloon, with its swinging doors and sawdust atmosphere, was recreated.

Today, the town is a mixture of the commercial and the magnificently historic. Pizza parlors, business offices, and new shops stand close by the Old Bird Cage Theater, where bullet holes still show daylight. The theater, built in 1881 as a combination theater and dance saloon, is one of several museums which will delight the heart of any Western fan. Here are some possessions of Doc Holliday as well as guns of the famous.

More on the order of a museum piece is the reconstructed O.K. Corral, where the gunfight is staged with wax figures. For the tourist market, guns still roar during three days set aside each year as "Helldorado Days." During this period, townspeople wear costumes of the 1880s and re-enact such doings as the gunfight of the O.K. Corral and the shooting of Marshal White.

Old Tucson, a movie set replica of the Old West

ABILENE, KANSAS

Abilene, today a rich and diversified agricultural community of more than 8000 persons, was once a booming cattle town which holds a colorful position in the annals of the Old West. In its day it was reputed to be the roughest, toughest, wildest town on the continent.

The town was founded in 1858 by Timothy F. Hersey and was given its Biblical name, city of the plains, by his wife. It was a rustic, slow-growing village when the Kansas Pacific Railroad chose to slice through it in 1867.

Its location at the end of the Texas cattle trail, the famed Chisholm Trail, made it for a time an ideal shipping point of cattle for the Eastern market. Before other towns became more advantageous shipping points, Abilene prospered as an open frontier town. Cowboys by the hundreds were paid their wages in Abilene at the conclusion of their parched and rigorous cattle drive along the trail. Stores, saloons and gambling houses were quickly erected to oblige those men who sought pleasurable means of ridding themselves of their sudden cash. During its heyday

between 1867 and 1871, more than three million head of cattle were shipped from Abilene. During much of the same period, Abilene was a pleasure and sin town where lawlessness reigned.

The townspeople in 1869 began a campaign for law and order by hiring Tom Smith as a marshal. Smith's reputation with the gun was such that both the law-abiding and the lawless complied quickly with his edict that no firearms would be permitted within the town. Smith kept the peace for a year—before he was gunned down—and was succeeded in his post by James Butler (Wild Bill) Hickok. Again, the town had the advantage of its marshal's enormous reputation with guns. Wild Bill's tenure in office ended in December 1871, coincident with the decline in Abilene's prosperity. But during that time Wild Bill, making the Alamo Saloon his headquarters and prowling the saloons along Texas Street, maintained law and order to a remarkable degree.

Today, Abilene attracts thousands of tourists for a number of reasons. Foremost is the Eisenhower Center, a memorial to President Dwight D. Eisenhower. The center consists of his boyhood home,

Gun fights were once common in Dodge City, Kansas

Fort Laramie, Wyoming, an Army post on the Oregon Trail

the Eisenhower Museum with its collection of war trophies, the Eisenhower Presidential Library and the All Faiths Meditation Chapel.

Another attraction is Old Abilene Town, a re-creation of early Abilene during the Wild Bill Hickok era. The re-creation was conceived by the Chamber of Commerce as a permanent memorial to early pioneers and was carried through by a specially chartered corporation, which financed the project through the sale of stock. Most of the buildings, located near the original townsite, are replicas of such establishments as the Merchants Hotel and the Alamo Saloon. A number of log structures, including a church and a homesteader's cabin, were located in other areas and moved to the site.

WICHITA, KANSAS

Wichita, largest city in Kansas, had its day in the Western sun as a major cattle shipping center for Texans. Cowboys, making their way along the tortuous Chisholm Trail, knew it as "Cowtown." This is the name given a re-creation of early Wichita, a civic project near Sim Memorial Park.

Cowtown began with a group effort to save one historic building and ended with the re-creation on an eighteen-acre site of an entire frontier day village.

The building was Wichita's first permanent church, erected in 1870 at a cost of $500 by the Presbyterian Congregation. The much-altered structure was up for sale in 1956 when a number of prominent citizens organized to buy and restore it. The success of this project led to organization of Historic Wichita, a non-profit corporation.

The organization acquired and restored 35 structures of historic importance. It rescued the Munger House, the town's first permanent dwelling, built of cottonwood logs welded together with plaster, sand and buffalo hair. It moved in Wyatt Earp's first Wichita jail with its rough timbers spiked together with square nails.

The restoration continued with Wichita's first drug store, a blacksmith shop, livery stable and first railway line and depot. The office of the first newspaper, the *Wichita City Eagle,* was re-created with equipment capable of turning out a newspaper in the old way.

Other buildings include the Buckhorn Bar, where a drunken cowboy is reputed to have silenced a music box with his six-gun, and the boyhood home of Billy the Kid.

9

That Old-Time Religion

*Above, Feast Hall at Old Economy
and, right, Rapp's Great House and church*

WITH ITS EARLY TRADITION of religious freedom, America was from the beginning a haven for persecuted minorities in Europe. It was to America that the Puritans, Quakers, Huguenots, Mennonites and many others turned to preserve their religious principles. It was also to America that scores of sects fled to establish their own utopias through communal living.

About 200 communal villages were established in America during the 18th and 19th centuries. A majority were founded by sects who sought withdrawal from a "sinful" world and regarded their members as a chosen people. Many of the sects believed in the imminent second coming of Christ.

In many of the utopian villages, the blazing light of purpose and dedication gutted within months. In others the torch burned brightly for decades due to strong leaders, such as George Rapp.

NEW HARMONY, INDIANA

"Father" George Rapp, a vinedresser and weaver, was one of a number of Pietists in Württemberg, Germany, who rebeled against the tenets of the state church and established their own religious doctrines. The resultant persecution by officials and conformist neighbors made life so intolerable and hazardous that the Pietists agreed to heed Rapp's plea for a move to America.

Rapp, as an emissary and scout, journeyed to Philadelphia in 1803 and found a forested tract of land in Butler County. On behalf of his followers he bought 3000 acres, now the village of Harmony, and the exodus of Pietists to the New World began.

Members of Rapp's Harmony Society were required to sign his Articles of Agreement, which placed all property in a common pool and provided for labor without pay. In return, the members were guaranteed full support for themselves and their families.

By 1806 there were 700 members in the community. Their industry and skill were such that buildings were quickly erected, farm land cleared, and shops hummed with new machinery. They produced for their own use and for sale such items as cloth, wagon harness, saddles and whisky. Their superior products at competitive prices found a ready market and money began to flow in.

Despite growing prosperity, the Harmonists were not content with the site of their village. They wanted land more suitable for vineyards and a location which would permit the shipment of their products by barge to broader market areas.

In 1815, the Rappites sold the entire community for $100,000 and moved to a new site on the Wabash River in Indiana. This became the village of New Harmony. The pattern of production was repeated, making the community the industrial pacemaker west of the Appalachians. Life jogged along pleasantly while Rapp built a church in the shape of a Greek cross, 125 feet in each direction, and his followers lived the good but celibate life.

The industry and ingenuity of the Harmonists may be judged by the houses they built, first of squared logs and later of brick. They developed a system of standardized building components, identifying framing members by number. When they built a house, they drew what components they needed from a common warehouse.

In 1824 Rapp, possibly feeling that his command over his flock was diminishing, helped shape a decision to abandon an entire town once more and to set up a new one. His followers packed their possessions and headed back to Pennsylvania to build their final and most elaborate town, Economy, north of Pittsburgh.

The New Harmony they left behind was given a new direction through Robert Owen, a Scottish industrialist who bought the town for $100,000. With 20,000 acres and 180 buildings under his control, Owen hoped to create his own utopia, his New View of Society. He was a self-made man to whom fortune came early in life, along with ideas which were radical for his day. His general aim was labor reform. To this end, he paid living wages at his textile mills in Scotland, subsidized workers during times of depression, and sold goods at cost at company stores. He was also a staunch believer in free schools for children of his employes.

In New Harmony Owen meant to demonstrate that a non-religious commune could be a success. He believed a village limited to 1200 persons could be self-sufficient in manufacture and agriculture and, at the same time, could reap sufficient profits to make a comfortable retirement at 50 compulsory.

Through newspaper advertisements, he invited those in sympathy with his cause to become a part of the village. Recruits by the hundreds flocked in, seeking the equality and golden opportunity that Owen promised. Unfortunately, skilled labor was scarce. The industries which had prospered under George Rapp barely creaked along. Dissatisfaction with the unfulfilled promise led to open dispute about the direction of the commune. Dissidents broke away by claiming portions of Owen's land and setting up their own communities. Within five years, Owen's noble experiment was conceded to be a failure. He returned to England and let the country find its own way under the capitalist system he deplored.

Nevertheless, the Owen contribution was a major one. He is credited with setting up in New Harmony the first kindergarten and the first free school system in America. He imported scientists and encouraged their efforts to such an extent that a number became renowned in the fields of conchology and geology.

Today, the town that has the distinction of being fostered by two experiments in communal living offers guided tours of buildings, a maze of boxwood hedges, and a walled cemetery which speak of the Rappite and Owen past. Among the buildings are the Rapp-Maclure Mansion, the Workingman's Institute with its museum and library, the Barrett Gate House Dormitory for Men and the Harmonist House.

AMBRIDGE, PENNSYLVANIA

Meanwhile, during the years Owen struggled to keep New Harmony alive, George Rapp and his followers farmed the land and set up new plants at Economy, making that community an industrial leader of its day.

More splendid than his others was George Rapp's Great House with 25 rooms and two wings. Still in the house is a vault in which the Harmonists once kept over $500,000 for emergency use. Larger than his others was Rapp's Feast Hall, a single room which could seat nearly 1000 per-

Feast Hall at Old Economy

sons during the Harmonists' special feasts, when men sat on the right side and women on the left. More exotic than his others was Rapp's Great House garden. It was described by the visiting Duke of Saxe-Weimar Eisenach in this way: "There is also a garden containing several acres with flowers and vegetables, as well as a vineyard, situated on a terrace-shaped half circle on the hill, ending in a bower. I especially admired the beautiful tulips of this garden, in the midst of which is a round basin with a noble spring."

Life jogged along pleasantly and industriously for the Harmonists until Rapp died in 1847 at the age of 90. Without his strength of leadership and with increasing industrial competition, the village began to decline economically. The decline was accelerated as the Harmonists dwindled in number through celibacy and a scarcity of new members. One by one, the once-humming industries shut down. Only the society investments in railroads, factories, land and lumber kept the aging Rappites in plenty.

The society was formally dissolved in 1905. Its property was sold to individuals except the Great House, which was preserved by the state as a museum. The museum, under the administration of the Pennsylvania Historical and Museum Commission, has since been expanded to embrace 6.7 acres of Old Economy village, the heart of the town.

Here are 17 buildings, all but five of them original and all but two on the original sites. Rapp's house with its bedrooms, two parlors, dining room and kitchen has been restored and furnished. The Harmonist Museum contains art works and scientific specimens they collected. On the walls of the Adult School are examples of Harmonist art and engineering work.

The village museum is designed to give you a complete picture of how the Harmonists lived and worked. The manner in which various products were made becomes apparent in the cabinetmakers' shop, the hat shop and the shoe store. Typical of the Harmonist dwellings is the Baker House, built of pre-cut lumber. The authentically furnished house has on display examples of pottery and other household articles produced by the Harmonists.

EPHRATA, PENNSYLVANIA

Predating the Harmonist experiment in communal life was another celibate community established at Ephrata, Pennsylvania, in 1732 by a group of German Pietists. Its leader was Conrad Beissel, a mystic who believed that communion with God could be found only through retirement from the world. Conrad Beissel's followers, inspired by his preaching, separated from the Dunkard Church (Church of the Brethren) to form their own church in their Rhenish homeland. In time, they followed him to America and the banks of Cocalico Creek.

Here they set up a monastic settlement with three orders, a brotherhood and a sisterhood, both of which practiced celibacy, and a married order of householders. So zealous was Beissel in his beliefs that he went on missionary journeys among the Pennsylvania Dutch, preaching, with little success, the superior blessedness of celibacy.

Perfection of body, soul and spirit was the goal of cloister members. They slept on narrow planks with wood blocks for pillows. They broke their rest with midnight services, marked by the ringing of bells and a torchlight procession. They built their structures without nails and with low, narrow doors—"straight is the gate and narrow the way."

The community, which at its height numbered 300, was a talented and industrious one. It had its own farms, mills and flocks, and it practiced household arts and crafts with great skill. Beginning in 1743, the Cloister press turned out great numbers of books and tracts, while the sisterhood produced magnificent hand-illuminated song books. Music was an important part of daily life. Beissel and others wrote scores of hymns, many of them sung today by the chorus of the Ephrata Cloister Associates, an organization which perpetuates the culture and arts of the sect.

Old Economy's storehouse

97

Community garden still blooms at Zoar

With Beissel's death in 1768, the community—like that of George Rapp—was rudderless. Its income dwindled, and by 1800 its celibate orders were virtually abandoned. In 1814 the remaining Cloister members spurned Beissel's doctrines by incorporating the Seventh Day German Baptist Church.

Beissel's influence and the manner of Cloister life are alive today, thanks to the Ephrata Cloister Associates, formed in cooperation with the Pennsylvania Historical and Museum Commission in 1957. The associates and the commission, dedicated to the restoration of the heart of the old community, have restored and furnished a complex of outstanding buildings, including the chapel, sisters' house, alms and bake house, cottages and an 1837 academy.

ZOAR STATE MEMORIAL, OHIO

The flight of George Rapp and his followers from the principality of Württemberg, Germany, to America was followed with great interest by many in the homeland. Among those who kept in touch with Rapp was Joseph Baumler, one of a group of Separatists who refused to embrace the Lutheran doctrine.

The pattern with the Separatists was comparable to that which Rapp had known some years before. These non-conformists were ignored, threatened and generally persecuted by church and state officials and by the community at large. With Rapp's example before them, the Separatists bought, sight unseen, a 5500-acre tract on the Tuscarawas River in Ohio. In 1817 Joseph Baumler led an advance party into the wilderness to prepare the land for the 300 members who were to follow.

This became the village of Zoar, which flourished with increasing income for 35 years under Baumler's direction. The first years were lean, and to cope with a general economic depression in the nation the Zoarites devised a communal system under which all property was placed in the hands of the Society of Separatists of Zoar. The society, in turn, dispensed all food and clothing and assigned to members their daily tasks.

Zoar, in time, prospered. Its geometrically laid out streets were lined with brightly colored homes with red tile roofs. Its community garden, laid out with geometric precision and symbolizing the New Jerusalem as described in Revelations, became a showplace. Its industries, including a brewery, turned out products which found a ready market.

Through the sale of farm implements, household utensils, stoves and other products, Zoar's treasury continued to fatten until Baumler's death in 1853. Without a strong leader the town's economy declined sharply. In March 1898 there was no other recourse but to formally dissolve the society and divide the remaining property and cash.

The state of Ohio subsequently acquired a number of historically significant buildings in Zoar and gave the task of restoring and furnishing them to the Ohio Historical Society. The Number One House, which was Joseph Baumler's residence, is a museum filled with prime examples of Zoarite arts and crafts. Other homes and structures offer a broad spectrum of Zoarite life.

AMANA COLONIES, IOWA

Even more financially successful than the communal ventures of George Rapp and Joseph Baumler was Amana Colonies, a related group of seven villages which survives today as a living community.

Like so many others, it was Germanic in origin. It owed its being to congregations of Inspirationists who shared common religious principles in the province of Hesse, Germany. The Inspirationists believed in the divinity of the Bible, holding that God revealed His wishes by messages transmitted through inspired prophets.

In the face of growing persecution, the Inspirationists learned through a divine message received by one of their number that survival depended on an exodus to America. The sect promptly dispatched four of its men to America to search for suitable land. When word arrived that the four agents had bought 5000 acres near Buffalo, New York, the exodus began in 1842.

The Inspirationists formed three villages in New York State and two on the Canadian side of the Niagara River. About 800 followers organized under the name of the Ebenezer Society and adopted laws which stated, among other things, that all property should be held in common.

The society prospered, making good use of its initial 5000 acres and another 5000 acres it later purchased. But it wanted more room for expansion. Another divine message dictated a search for land to the west. Dutifully, a committee explored the prairies of Iowa and submitted its report. A later committee returned to Iowa to buy

18,000 acres of land. Little by little, the New York land was sold at a profit while society members moved to the new site over a 10-year period. The first village, Amana, was laid out on a hill north of the Iowa River in 1855. Six other villages were subsequently staked out in the form of an oval from one to three miles apart.

In its new location, the Community of True Inspiration was incorporated under the name of Amana Society. Its aim continued to be devotion to its faith and a striving for spiritual purification. Each village, governed by its own board of elders, had its own farmland, shops and mills to tend. While families had their own living quarters, they shared meals in large community kitchen-houses. The sexes were separated for meals, as they were for religious services in their plain meeting houses.

The society was not concerned about making a profit through its factories, meat shops and other enterprises. But profit came its way as visitors made the quality of the Amana products known.

Amana continued as a closely-knit, restricted community until the impact of the 20th century began to make inroads on its culture. The radio and the automobile brought members into close touch with fast developments in the America

Bedroom at Amana

Amana bakery

about them, awakening in the younger generation a wish to be a part of the land beyond.

In the face of this awakening, the leaders of the society brought to fruition a plan of modernization, bringing about the separation of religious and temporal affairs. Industry became a separate entity under The Amana Society, while religion became the concern of the Amana Church Society. This separation brought rapid changes. Community kitchens and dining halls were abandoned. Children were encouraged to attend colleges outside Amana. And, by the end of 1935, every dwelling was individually owned.

Today, Amana industry is largely known through its home freezers, refrigerators and room air conditioners. But its traditions continue in everyday life, and much of what was Amana past is preserved in its restored homes and shops.

You may visit the seven closely allied villages, which have been established as a National Historic Landmark, and note the manner in which the old and the new world blend. Still in operation are the original Amana enterprises, the woolen mills, the farms, the cabinet shops and the bakeries. But today these are industries run under the impetus of private enterprise.

Museum homestead reflects life at Amana

HANCOCK SHAKER VILLAGE, MASSACHUSETTS

Five miles west of Pittsfield, the United Society of Believers, called Shakers, established a farming community in 1790. This was the third of 19 such communities founded by the Shakers and one which, at its peak in the 1830s, housed some 300 adults.

The Shakers were a sect of religious dissenters, spun off in their own direction during England's 1747 Quaker revival. The sect's method of worship, which included meditation, shaking and singing, brought it its name of "Shaking Quakers," later shortened to Shakers.

Its leader in America was Mother Ann Lee, a former mill hand and cook in Manchester, England, who brought her gospel to New York in 1774 and quickly gathered converts by the hundreds. She advocated the simple life and celibacy, preaching that "concupiscence" was the great sin and the source of the world's wrongs. She preached with such conviction in New York State and in New England that new Shaker villages continued to form after her death in 1784. The converts adopted her creed of plain dress, thrift, efficiency and equality of the sexes.

The Shaker doctrine seemed to appeal to the farmers, mechanics and tradesmen who had skills to offer in their new environment. As a result, the Shakers were recognized as an ingenious sect, credited with inventing the first circular saw, the common clothespin, the metal nib for pens and the chimney cap. They redesigned buildings to achieve the greatest efficiency possible in washing, heating, ventilating and cleaning. Their products, always of the highest quality and invariably without ornamentation, found markets easily. The typical Shaker village had three "families," or units under the ministration of an elder. Each family was housed in one or more large dwellings and maintained its own shops, livestock, barns and fields.

Celibacy was the keyword, with men and women forbidden to speak to each other unless a third party was present. It was inevitable, as the number of recruits from the outside world dwindled, that the movement would one day come to a halt.

The community in Hancock folded in 1960 when only three Shakers remained. When the property of nearly 1000 acres was placed on the market, a number of public-spirited citizens sought to preserve the village and formed Shaker Community, Inc., for this purpose. The organization bought the land and began restoration of 19 structures with the aim of fully and accurately depicting the enduring values of Shaker character, culture and workmanship.

Restoration has been completed on most buildings, including a four-story brick Church Family Dwelling built in 1830 to house a hundred men and women, and a round barn with three interior levels arranged for efficiently and cleanly servicing from a central core the many cow stalls that line the perimeter. Shaker life and industry are brought to life through exhibits and furnishings in such buildings as the Sisters' shop, laundry and machine shop, ministry wash house, and ice house.

CANTERBURY, NEW HAMPSHIRE

During our visit to the Shaker Village in Canterbury during the summer of 1969, we rang the bell of the two-story brick office, gift shop and residence, still occupied by Shakers, and were greeted by Sister Lillian Phelps. She wore the familiar bonnet of the Shakers and an ankle-length gown, and on her comparatively smooth face was the unmistakable cast of serenity.

One of six sisters in residence, Sister Lillian, was 92, although she looked no more than 65. Her longevity, like that of most Shakers, was due, she said, to her belief in God and in the Shaker way of life. She was 16 and had the firm intention of continuing her study of the piano at a conservatory when she came to Canterbury for a summer vacation. By summer's end, her enthusiasm for Shaker life was such that she didn't want to leave it. She didn't.

Across the road from the office like a freshly painted ghost town, the white frame structures, once home to as many as 400 Shakers, were untenanted. Gardens laid out more than a century ago still bloomed. Fields, once scythed by 40 men keeping pace with each other in a long row, looked out at tall hills and peaceful valleys.

Free to wander about the village, we headed for the Meetinghouse along a broad, grassy mall, where carriages of churchgoers were once tied up. The mall is lined with massive sugar maple trees planted as saplings in the 1850s. Each tree was nurtured by and named for a homeless child, adopted by the Shakers, making the mall, in effect, a memorial to orphans.

On one side of the mall is a row of two-story buildings, each with a raised porch squarely in the middle. Here were the Infirmary where medicines derived from roots and herbs were dispensed and the sisters' dwelling, with living rooms and sleeping apartments on two floors. Largest of the 18 buildings is the Big Dwelling House, erected in 1793. Most of its 56 rooms were used as sleeping apartments. In the kitchen on the basement level two sisters were cooks for four weeks, changing with others at the end of that time.

Non-residential buildings include a number which yielded an income for the Shakers. Sweaters and hose were made on the second floor of a laundry building. Sisters made cloaks and shirts of fine flannel on home-made sewing desks in the sewing shops. A barn, 250 feet long and the largest in the state, once housed more than a hundred head of registered Guernsey stock.

The Meetinghouse, built in 1792, has an entrance on the right for women and on the left for men. It was one of seven built for Shaker villages by Brother Moses Johnson, who insulated the structure with moss and birch bark.

The Meetinghouse, where dancing or marching was part of the early religious services, now houses

Brick homes in Shakertown

objects and memorabilia which are a testament to Shaker industry and inventiveness. Displayed along walls and on tables are such inventions and devices as a folding stereoscopic viewer, and apple-paring machine, a box stove and tilting chairs. Here, too, are the scores of different brooms and brushes the Shakers made and sold, along with sewing boxes and many types of baskets.

Visitors today may enter the museum for a moderate charge and may wander about the grounds. The hope of the sisters is that restoration will one day return the village to its original luster. To this end they have formed Shaker Village, Incorporated, a non-profit organization which has begun a program of restoration and expansion.

PLEASANT HILL, KENTUCKY

The last of three Shaker communities which are museum villages is Shakertown, situated high above the palisades of the Kentucky River near Harrodsburg, Kentucky. This village of 23 original buildings was founded in 1805, reached its 500-member peak in the mid-1800s and expired in 1910.

There were three families at Pleasant Hill, each with its own houses, shops, farming lands and orchards. Their industry was such that it was not unusual for them to produce 500 pairs of shoes, put up over 4000 jars of sweetmeats and dry a winter's supply of apples in a year. This was in addition to their weaving, spinning, sewing and production of such craft items as willow baskets, palm-leaf bonnets and fine cedar pails.

Restoration of the village began in April 1968 by the non-profit organization of Shakertown, which acquired 2250 acres of the original Shaker lands. Center for the restoration is the Family Dwelling House, once the home of 50 men and women and now a museum of Shaker handicrafts.

What makes Pleasant Hill different from other restorations is that visitors are invited to spend the night in "retiring rooms," furnished as they were in Shaker times. The 56 available retiring rooms, however, have been updated with new plumbing and other conveniences.

NEW PHILADELPHIA, OHIO

The Moravian Church in 18th century America was concerned about the Indian and his education. It wanted to improve the Indian's lot by teaching him such subjects as writing, reading, agricultural techniques and handicrafts.

It sent missionaries among the Indians as early as 1734 and established several mission villages in Pennsylvania some years later. Its desire to expand its area of activity was such that it dispatched missionary David Zeisberger in May 1772 to Tuscarawas Valley in Ohio to blaze a new missionary trail. Zeisberger had with him 28 Christian Indians who were immediately put to work clearing the land and building a mission house. His forces were strengthened by the arrival of two other missionaries, John Heckewelder and John Ettwein, with an additional 200 converts.

The expanded force cleared the land and established the village of Schoenbrunn, laying out 40 lots in the shape of a T. Within a few years the village had more than 60 log dwellings in addition to a number of general-use structures. It was their misfortune that Schoenbrunn was located between the warring British and American armies during the Revolutionary War, each army with its Indian allies. The village was constantly harassed by both forces. Fearing for their lives, the missionaries rallied their converts and departed for safer havens in 1777.

With time, fire and neglect leveled the structures and made the mission a forgotten chapter of history until the 1920s. It was then that the state of Ohio acquired the site and the Ohio Historical Society took over its administration. The land was excavated to rescue artifacts and to determine the location of the various Moravian structures. The well-researched re-creation of a single cabin in 1927 was followed gradually by the reconstruction of a church, school, and 13 other structures.

BETHLEHEM, PENNSYLVANIA

A settlement which grew to become the booming steel town of Bethlehem, Pennsylvania, was established on the banks of the Lehigh River by a small group of the old Protestant sect of Moravians in 1741. Bethlehem rapidly expanded as a Moravian center with the establishment of a Moravian College, still flourishing. So sturdily built were the early homes and shops that many of them stand today in the old heart of the city,

Furnishings and costumes are authentic at Shakertown, Kentucky

providing a representative picture of the early village.

The Central Moravian Church, which owns many of the structures, maintains a number of buildings as museums and provides guides for a long walking tour. The tour will take you to the Annie S. Kemerer Museum, comprised of the Brethren's House and the Main Hall. The house was once the residence and shop area for single men of the Moravian community while the Main Hall, built in 1854, houses restored Victorian rooms. Along the tour is the Moravian Cemetery where gravestones are laid flat, indicating that all men are equal in the sight of God; the Gemein Haus, oldest structure in the city; and the Central Moravian Church, built in 1803.

Portions of the old village are being restored by Historic Bethlehem, Incorporated, an organization concerned with archaeological and archival research into the 18th century industrial quarter of the city. In addition to its restoration, the organization has preserved a number of industrial buildings, still used for the functions for which they were constructed a century ago.

OLD SALEM, NORTH CAROLINA

The history of the Moravians may also be traced in Old Salem, a restored Moravian Congregation town in Winston-Salem. Here you may inspect the façades of many old or reconstructed buildings and browse through eight exhibition buildings open to the public.

Salem, a planned community founded in 1766, was operated as a congregation town in which the business life as well as the spiritual life of all residents was directed by the church. The town soon gained renown as an industrial and educational center. In the mid-19th century, a new town—the county seat, Winston—began to thrive north of Salem, and the old community became subordinate to the new one.

The Moravian heritage remained entrenched through the decades in buildings built by master craftsmen. Many so withstood the test of time that

America's oldest tobacco shop stands in Old Salem

they continued to stand solidly at the end of World War II. But the heart of Old Salem had so altered with time that it was a decaying area.

With so many old buildings ready for demolition, it seemed to a grocery store owner in 1947 to be the logical spot for a supermarket. The announcement of his plans kicked up a storm among preservationists. They not only stalemated those plans, but perservered as a citizen group to form a non-profit corporation three years later, Old Salem, Incorporated.

With more than $6 million gained through private donations, the organization acquired over 80 properties in the historic area, restored more than 30 of them and demolished about a hundred structures. Utility wires were placed underground and street signs redesigned to conform to the original style. Through traffic has been diverted to a four-lane bypass at the edge of Old Salem. A number of buildings, restored or reconstructed on the outside, were adapted on the inside for use as dwellings, shops and offices.

Tours with costumed guides are available for groups, while trained hostesses remain on duty in the exhibit buildings. These are imposing structures, representative of the major buildings in the old town. The Single Brothers House, built in two sections in 1769 and 1786, was home for the unmarried men of the town. It was also here that boys of 14 came to live and learn a craft. The Miksch Tobacco Shop (1771) was the first privately owned house in Salem and is the oldest tobacco shop still standing in America. A boarding school for boys now houses the antiques collection of the Wachovia Historical Society and an exhibit of Moravian musical instruments and manuscripts. Also serving as a museum is the Salem Tavern (1784), first brick structure in Salem.

Other exhibit buildings include the John Vogler House, the brick residence of a silversmith and clockmaker; the Winkler Bakery, which was home and livelihood for the Winkler family for more than a century; and the Market-Fire House, a fire station which doubled as a market for the sale of meat.

NAUVOO, ILLINOIS

Nauvoo, Illinois, today a small and tranquil town on the banks of the Mississippi River, was once the largest community in the state and the principal Mormon center in the country. A restored portion of the town concentrates on the Mormon past.

The spread of the Mormon Church was rapid in the years after 1827, when prophet Joseph Smith published his Book of Mormon. Mormon centers sprang up first in New York State and then in regions as far west as Missouri. The town of Far West in Caldwell County, Missouri, became the principal center and might have remained so except for a revelation announced by prophet Joseph. He had a divine message, he said, that the Mormon "saints" were to take over all the land in the area. This pronouncement did not sit well with non-Mormon land owners. Their initial indignation and fear turned to outrage and open violence.

In the face of increasing hostility, more than 15,000 Mormons pulled up stakes in Missouri and headed for Illinois. In 1839 they began to build Nauvoo into a New Jerusalem, with a gigantic Mormon temple in its center. The town prospered and spread with the construction of homes, shops, schools and a newspaper building. Mormons and non-Mormons swelled the population to more than 20,000.

Prayer Hall at Old Salem

Mansion House in Nauvoo was an early Mormon center

Again prophet Joseph created a rift through the announcement of another divine message. This message was to the effect that polygamy should henceforth be an accepted practice. The prospect of a polygamous community horrified many residents and was soundly denounced by the newspaper, *The Expositor.* When a mob broke into the newspaper building and destroyed its presses, the Mormons were immediately suspect.

Nauvoo became a city divided. Clashes between Mormons and non-Mormons reached such proportions that the state militia moved in. Joseph Smith and his brother, Hyrum, accused of taking part in the destruction of the newspaper press, were imprisoned in nearby Carthage. Here, on June 22, 1844, a mob broke into their cells and murdered both men. Despite their deaths, hostility and violence continued. Two years later, the Mormons once more pulled up stakes, this time moving west across the plains to the valley of the Great Salt Lake.

With the Mormon exodus, Nauvoo was a shadow of its former self. Houses were boarded up and shops closed down. In 1849 a group of Frenchmen and Germans, calling themselves the "Pioneers of Humanity," or "Icarians," moved in with the hope of setting up a utopian colony. Within a few years another utopian dream turned to dust. Nauvoo, shrunken in size, began to assume its present character as a small community.

Today, along quiet streets, you may visit such Mormon residences as the Brigham Young home and the Joseph Smith homestead. Guides will explain to you the significance of more than 30 historic sites, reminders not only of Mormon enterprise but of that of the Icarians, whose utopia shattered in the making.

BISHOP HILL, ILLINOIS

Erik Jansson, a farmer in Bishop Hill, Sweden, disputed the tenets of the Swedish Lutheran Church and in the early 1840s tried to change them by preaching his own views about the countryside. He succeeded in converting many listeners to his beliefs. He also succeeded in incurring the increasing wrath of the church.

To escape the latter, he fled to America, bought 40 acres of land in Illinois and announced his intention to set up a communal village. In 1846 about 800 of his followers left their homes for the promise of religious freedom in America, thereby establishing the first major Swedish settlement in the Midwest.

The original 40 acres became hundreds. Shops were built, cattle were tended and land was tilled. The colonists lived in communal buildings, ate together in a dining hall which seated 1000 persons and worked at their assigned tasks. For a time the village prospered with the sale of brooms, linen, furniture and dairy products. But the ideals of the colonists became less sharp after Jansson's death in 1850. Dissident groups withdrew from the society, taking with them their lands and possessions. The supervision of the village under a seven-man board was such that the community went deeply into debt.

A contemporary writer in the 1870s found Bishop Hill *"slowly falling into decay. The houses are still mostly inhabited; there are several shops; but the larger buildings are out of repair; and business has centered at Galva, five or six miles distant.... On the whole, it is a melancholy story."*

Bishop Hill as a communal venture was dissolved in 1891 after much bitter debate and all property held in common was divided among its members. The town declined in population but adapted itself increasingly to American life. The Jansson years were a distant bit of history when the town in the early 1960s decided to restore the original Swedish settlement and to preserve its Scandinavian heritage.

Open for your inspection is the Colony Church, a white frame structure begun in 1848 which could seat 1000 persons. Housed in the church are exhibits of colony tools, art works and other artifacts.

Some early buildings, fashioned of brick, were designed in the Greek Revival style. Among these is the Steeple Building, which today houses a museum and a shop specializing in handcrafts. The gamut of restored structures ranges from a store and post office to a blacksmith shop, which has been converted into an antique shop.

Colony Church at Bishop Hill can seat 1,000 persons

Furnace at Batsto provided cannons for General Washington

10

Iron, Lumber and Farm Villages

THE GROWTH OF A COUNTRY can be related directly to the abundance of its natural resources and the expansion of its industries. The first colonists found in great abundance land which they could farm and timber which they could mill for export. Vital for their existence and economic well-being was the establishment of an ironworks to diminish their dependence on distant Europe for iron products. A number of industrial villages in the United States dramatize the manner in which our forefathers produced iron, felled tall timber, and farmed the land.

The need for domestic iron was evident from the time of the first settlements. The necessary ingredients for its production were iron ore, limestone as a fluxing material, charcoal as fuel and water power; the existence in America of all these was known as early as 1585 when Sir Walter Raleigh noted iron ore in the bogs of North Carolina.

There were attempts to smelt iron in Virginia during the 1620s, but it was not until 1646 that the first successful ironworks was established at Saugus, Massachusetts, a community 10 miles north of Boston. Today, the Saugus Ironworks Restoration, recognized as the birthplace of America's iron and steel industry, is a historic landmark. The Saugus ironworks remained in operation until about 1670 when the supply of

raw materials began to run out and the availability of labor diminished. The structures in time disintegrated and vanished, but the historic significance of that first iron industry was not forgotten.

The iron and steel industry and the First Iron Works Association after years of extensive research reconstructed the industrial complex at a cost of more than $1.5 million and opened it as a museum in 1954. The ironworks on the banks of the Saugus River is comparable in its physical design to hundreds of others which flourished for a time in states along the Eastern seaboard. The buildings at Saugus, staffed by costumed guides, will reveal to you the complex nature of smelting iron and the number of skills required.

The process called for the ready availability of great stands of timber. Trees were needed to provide a constant supply of charcoal and some furnaces consumed nearly an acre of forest for a day's operation. Cordwood was stacked in pits and charred by slow, carefully tended fires. The fuel was then stored in charcoal houses from which it was later hauled to the nearby furnace. The furnace, walled with local stone, was distinguished by its large stack. A water wheel worked the bellows which provided the necessary blast for the furnace. Into the inner chamber of the furnace iron ore, charcoal and limestone were dumped in layers. The limestone combined with impurities in the ore, permitting molten iron to run off into casting beds of sand.

A separate building housed the forge where pig iron was reheated and, through blows of a heavy forge hammer, refined into bar iron. The iron was converted into bars or rods, preparatory to its final shaping into products by a blacksmith.

In common with other ironworks, Saugus has an elaborate residence which was home for the ironmaster or plant manager. The ironmaster, always regarded as the top of the social scale, invariably lived an elegant life, his Big House maintained by a staff of servants.

While the Saugus reconstruction remains an industrial museum, the extent to which iron plantations became virtually self-sustaining communities is apparent in museum villages located in New Jersey and Pennsylvania.

ALLAIRE, NEW JERSEY

New Jersey, wedged between the Hudson and Delaware Rivers, turned to industry for its economic well-being early in its history. Its heartland, the Pine Barrens, was rich in rivers and streams for water power and rich in bog ore from which iron could be extracted.

The first iron venture was launched in 1674. Other forges and furnaces were set up early in the 18th century and, at the time of the Revolution, there were nearly a hundred plants producing iron products.

Some closed in the depression years which followed the Revolution. Others continued to operate, using charcoal for fuel, until the mid-19th century. It was then that the discovery of coal in Pennsylvania's Alleghenies made the New Jersey production unprofitable. Western Pennsylvania became the center of the iron industry, and New Jersey's iron-producing communities were largely abandoned.

The Deserted Village at Allaire, a part of Allaire State Park, was in its heyday a self-sufficient community of more than 500 persons with its own ironworks, church, store and dwellings. This was home to woodchoppers, firemen, blacksmiths and molders. And from this community came such products as pots, pans, Franklin stoves and whale oil kettles.

The village was little more than woodland in 1813 when the Monmouth Furnace was erected. Nine years later, James P. Allaire of New York bought the furnace, some 5000 acres of land and more than 20 structures for $19,000. The ironworks

became his source for pig iron needed for the marine engine shops he operated in New York.

Allaire was a humanitarian as well as an industrialist. He supervised expansion of the village, provided a church for worship and a teacher for the education of children. His influence on the town was strong until 1846, when the decline of the bog iron industry forced him to board up the furnace.

Allaire was a ghost town when Arthur Brisbane, a newspaper editor, bought the village and 5000 acres of land as the site of his country home. It was Brisbane's hope, before his death in 1936, that the state might be persuaded to turn the village into a state park. His hope became reality in 1941 when the state accepted from Brisbane's widow a gift of land including the village.

The long work of restoration began, and today the village is a period piece, recalling its early days of prosperity. Many of the buildings are more than museums. Saddle horses may be rented at the restored stable. Antiques are on sale at the old carpenter shop. Gifts may be purchased at the renovated general store.

The tallest building is the country store, a four-story brick structure with iron lintels. A boarding house with a three-story brick addition, built in 1835, boasts 25 rooms and a massive dining room. Unique in its design is the church that Allaire built, its steeple not over the front entrance but at the rear.

BATSTO, NEW JERSEY

Larger and more ambitious than the restoration of the Deserted Village at Allaire is the restoration of the colonial village of Batsto, established as a bog-iron-producing community in 1766. This was a town of nearly 1000 persons, playing an important part in the industrial development of the United States. It furnished the American forces with cannon and ball and with other essential iron items during the Revolution. Its productivity was such that ironworkers were exempted from military service.

Ten years after it began operation on the Batsto River, the furnace was pouring out a great volume of iron products which were touted in newspaper advertisements as *"a great variety of iron pots, kettles, Dutch ovens, and oval fish kettles, either with or without covers, skillets of different sizes, being much lighter, neat and superior in quality to any imported from Great Britain."*

The furnace switched to munitions and other articles of war during the Revolution. A wartime letter noted, *"The furnace has begun her blast and is now running entirely on shot and shells on a contract with the board of war for about 100 tons."*

Prosperity continued in post-Revolution years, and the furnace again produced ball and shot during the War of 1812. By 1829, production was averaging 800 tons of iron a year, chiefly in the form of castings.

Pennsylvania's growing status as an iron producer dampened Batsto's operation in the late 1830s, and closed down the furnace in 1848. The village hopefully turned to glass-making as a substitute industry, but that operation prospered for less than a decade. Workers sought employment elsewhere, buildings were abandoned. The coup d'état was a fire in 1874 which destroyed nearly half the workers' houses. The buildings which remained were silent and neglected until 1954 when the state bought 56,000 acres of land around Batsto and later added a tract of 40,000 acres. Aided by history-oriented organizations, the state in 1958 launched a restoration program.

Today, the grist mill is in operation, capable of milling corn and wheat. The 1882 sawmill can produce cedar shingles and siding. The blacksmith and wheelwright's shop has been restored and equipped. The Batsto of yesteryear, with its furnace and its glassworks, is again alive.

CORNWALL, PENNSYLVANIA

As early as 1727, iron furnaces began to dot the Pennsylvania countryside, while around them sprouted miners' villages. A few, like the furnace at Cornwall, established in 1742, are preserved as examples of the enterprise which laid the foundations for Pennsylvania's complex iron and steel industry of today.

The Cornwall furnace supplied George Washington's Continental Army with cannon, shells and stoves, drawing a large part of its labor force from Hessian soldiers captured by American troops.

The furnace was built by Peter Grubb, who migrated with his father from Cornwall, England, in the 1720s. During the 1730s, he coupled his discovery in Cornwall, Pennsylvania, of magnetic ore banks and limestone with his knowledge of mining operations and realized the industrial potential of the area.

Ore buggies in Cornwall's museum building

Cornwall Furnace operated for 141 years

He acquired land, including the Cornwall Ore Banks, a rich source of iron ore, and established the furnace which remained in operation for 141 years. Nearby, Grubb built a village for miners and their families.

In 1798 the property came under the control of Robert Coleman, who also owned the Hopewell and Colebrook forges and Elizabeth Furnace. Long after it ceased operation the furnace remained in the Coleman family until a great-granddaughter gave the plant to the Commonwealth in 1932.

The furnace is today maintained as a museum by the Pennsylvania Historical Commission. The mines discovered by Peter Grubb are owned by the Bethlehem Steel Company and are still in operation. The workers still occupy the stone houses of the 19th century miners' village nearby.

HOPEWELL, PENNSYLVANIA

Of all the iron-making villages open to you, the most far-ranging is Hopewell, Pennsylvania, a National Historic Site maintained by the National Park Service. President Franklin D. Roosevelt set aside the charcoal burning cold-blast furnace and its surrounding village on August 3, 1938, as representative of those villages which made iron during the 18th and 19th centuries. The village offers an authentic picture of social, cultural, economic and industrial life in an early iron-making community.

Hopewell Forge was built about 1744 by William Bird, a New Jersey iron tycoon, as a small part of his expanding iron and land empire. Until his death in 1761, Bird was responsible for construction of a number of forges and furnaces, at the same time acquiring tracts of land which eventually contained about 3000 acres. A son, Mark Bird, carried on the family enterprise and erected the present Hopewell Furnace on French Creek, near Birdsboro, in 1770–71.

Mark Bird's concern for the American cause during the Revolutionary War was stronger than his concern for his industrial empire. As a colonel in the Berks County militia, he used his own funds to fit out 300 men of his battalion with uniforms, tents and provisions. He geared his ironworks, gristmills and sawmills to wartime production, turning out supplies for the Continental Army. His dedication to the American cause was such that he emerged from the war with heavy debts. The debts and the operating costs of his industries stripped him of his wealth. In April 1788 he was forced to relinquish the Hopewell property to partially satisfy claims against him.

Hopewell in later years had a succession of owners and its share of ups and downs, savoring its greatest period of prosperity in the years after

Skillets and kettles were cast in Hopewell's Casthouse

Charcoal pit is fired annually at Hopewell

1800. It was during those years that a stamping mill was built to salvage iron from the slag, and a resmelting furnace was added to increase the output of small castings. Its annual tonnage of pig iron rose from 252 in 1800 to 533 in 1824. Its castings supplied the Philadelphia market with a variety of products, including stoves and fireplaces.

The depression of 1837 and the rise of Western Pennsylvania as an iron center were death-dealing blows for Hopewell. By 1845 it had discontinued its finished castings and concentrated on pig iron, but competition proved too strong. The furnace was blown out for the last time in 1883, making it one of the last of the old cold-blast furnaces to die.

The National Park Service has restored the village to the 1820–40 period, its peak production years. Visitors can prepare themselves for the journey into the industrial past by first taking in the Visitor Center. Here you may watch an orientation slide program and browse through a museum which outlines the techniques of iron production.

Great strides in the restoration have been made since 1955 when a blacktop road which cut through the village was removed. Amish carpenters provided the skill for most of the restoration projects. The group of ironmaking buildings were completed after extensive research; dwellings and shops have been restored and furnished in period; personnel are costumed. In a different way and in a new era, the life of the village goes on and charcoal fires glow once more.

EAU CLAIRE, WISCONSIN

Lumber has long been and continues to be a precious commodity. It was an important fuel for the early iron industry and, with Europe's dwindling forests, a valuable export item. With the westward expansion of the United States, the exploitation of virgin timberland made great fortunes for many lumber barons.

From the 1820s on, the millions of acres of fine timberland in the Great Lakes region sparked a boom that lasted through the century. Lumbermen by the thousands swarmed into Wisconsin, Michigan and Northern Illinois, felling trees which were floated in lake and river waters to sawmills.

The rough, tough lumbermen were a breed apart, working long days and sleeping short nights. Working in isolated areas, they turned to tall tales for diversion, creating such whopping folk legends as Paul Bunyan, who reputedly could cut the pine

off 40 acres at a single swing of the ax, and his giant blue ox, Babe, who reversed the current of the Mississippi by taking one long, cool drink.

In the 1880s, there were more than 100,000 men working the Great Lakes pineries—and steadily stripping the region of its forests. It is this facet of American life that you can visualize at Eau Claire, Wisconsin, where the Paul Bunyan Camp immortalizes a way of life that is gone forever. The 40-man lumber camp was conceived in 1922 and later erected by the Eau Claire Kiwanis Club as a memorial to the pioneer lumbermen. It is now maintained by the city as a well-researched replica of a typical logging camp of the late 1890s.

You will learn here that a "dingle," a covered walkway between the cook shanty and the bunkhouse, was originally used to store foodstuffs that would survive the open air. Eau Claire's dingle is a museum devoted largely to a collection of log ends, with stamps and bark marks identifying the owners of the felled timber, much as cattle were branded in the West.

The cook shanty, which doubled as bedroom for the cook and his helper, is an exhibit area for cooking implements, logging pictures and maps. Descriptive matter here will tell you it was traditional that woodsmen take their meals at the same place in which they were first served and that the lumber crew ate in comparative silence, speeding their return to their tasks.

The bunkhouse is furnished with two tiers of bunks and a rude bench, extending from one end of the room to the other. Other pieces include a wooden wash trough, the camp account desk and a medicine chest with typical remedies of the time.

A stable has stalls for oxen as well as horses, both of which carted logs to the waterway. The outdoor shed house is a museum of logging sleighs, jammer apparatus and a bateau, a boat used on the river during log drives.

LANCASTER, PENNSYLVANIA

The first essentials of the colonists in America were shelter and food. Forests were cleared to provide farm land, seed was hopefully sown and its fruition as a crop led to rejoicing and general thanksgiving. From the beginning, agriculture was an important industry. It remains so today, using mechanized and computerized techniques.

The farm villages in the nation, like the Pennsylvania Farm Museum of Landis Valley at Lancaster, are a measure of the progress of agricultural equipment and life. This museum consists of a

Paul Bunyan is as big as life in Lumbertown, Minnesota

group of representative buildings housing exhibits of various facets of rural life. It is intended to depict rural Pennsylvania "from the age of homespun to the Gay Nineties."

The museum stemmed from a collection of rural Americana, amassed from the 1880s by two brothers, Henry Landis, an engineer and writer, and George Landis, an engineer. Their family farm inspired the common interest, and it was on the family farm they opened their museum in 1925. Their collection at that time consisted of well over 100,000 antique items, including a wide range of farm implements. They went to great pains to place the antiques in period buildings in which they might have belonged. Fifteen years later, the Landis Valley Museum was incorporated to administer the project and to expand it. The Pennsylvania Historical and Museum Commission took over the museum village in 1953 and expanded its inventory to more than 250,000 items.

Farm implements, craft tools and household arts are not only preserved but are demonstrated. A period tavern is the center for a collection of folk art. A Conestoga wagon, the "prairie schooner" which helped to settle the West, has a place of honor in the wagon shed. An old-fashioned country store is in business near a row of period craft shops.

The museum represents a number of distinct periods. The Landis brothers' home, for example, is a fine example of a Victorian farmhouse, while an early 19th century group of buildings reflects the Federal period of design.

TALLAHASSEE, FLORIDA

Aimed primarily at youngsters is the Junior Museum and Pioneer Farm, a historical restoration which opened in Tallahassee, Florida, in 1962. This is centered around an arrangement of four museum buildings connected by covered porches at Lake Bradford. Exhibits buildings cover the natural sciences, the social sciences, art and music.

What sets the museum apart is a complex of log buildings, built in the 1880s and moved from their original sites to make up a miniature farm community. The area, enclosed by a split rail fence, includes a reconstructed smokehouse and a blacksmith shop. Seven other buildings, including a log cabin, have been furnished with tools and other equipment of the period. What's more, the barnyard is the province of all the animals you would expect to see at a typical farm.

11

A Word on Walking Tours

Old Court House, New Castle, Delaware

THROUGHOUT THE COUNTRY scores of communities have awakened to the fact that within their boundaries they possess significant landmarks and historic sites which eloquently tell a portion of the American story. Where buildings and sites are scattered, it is only through a walking tour that they achieve their greatest meaning. The walking tour has become, in effect, a means of examining and assessing important portions of the yesterday of the community. The tour has become an accepted and well-mapped device which will tell the wanderer what the issues were and who the important men were in other centuries.

All the walking tours have their individual stories to tell. In Boston, Massachusetts, the Freedom Trail speaks eloquently of the days of the Revolution. The graves of John Hancock, Paul Revere, and the martyrs of the Boston Massacre are marked by weathered stones in the Granary Burying Ground. The Boston Tea Party was plotted in the Old South Meeting House. From the old belfry of Old North Church Paul Revere is said to have gotten the lantern signal to start his famous ride.

In Maine, the Portland History Trail charted by the Greater Portland Chamber of Commerce sheds light on many eras and many personalities. The

Portland Headlight, built in 1791, was the first lighthouse to be authorized by the United States and is the oldest lighthouse in operation. Fort Gorges, which can be seen from the Eastern Promenade, was begun in pre-Civil War days to protect the inner harbor. Open houses along the way include one built in 1755 by George Tate, mast agent for the British Navy, the childhood home of Henry Wadsworth Longfellow, and the Victoria Mansion with its period architecture and furnishings.

Just as museum villages provide a compact, concentrated view of early America, many a walking tour provides a spread-out but integrated perspective on the shaping of our nation. Here is a sampling of some of the more significant walking tours within the United States.

DELAWARE

Walking tours in the early and historic towns of Dover and New Castle take on added meaning and charm once a year when privately owned residences are open to the public and townspeople in period costume serve as guides.

Dover, created by order of William Penn and laid out in 1717, celebrates "Old Dover Days" on the first Saturday and Sunday in May. Focal point of the celebration is the Green where early markets, fairs and slave markets were held. Ranged about the Green are distinguished homes and such public buildings as the Old State House, second oldest in the United States. Its Old Bell of 1763 was used to summon "the freeholders of Kent at the Court House in the town of Dover, to take into consideration the acts of the British Parliament in shutting up the Port of Boston."

Three of the recommended 29 points of interest are buildings of the Delaware State Museum. In one of the buildings is a group of structures—a Swedish-type log house, a grist mill, blacksmith shop, and cobbler's exhibit—which reflect life in the colonial days.

New Castle, founded in 1651 by the Dutch, holds its "Day in Old New Castle" on the third Saturday in May. It has an impressive list of 52 points of interest, headed by the dignified buildings which served as Delaware's colonial capital and first state house. The spire atop the State House was used as the radius of the 12-mile circle which formed the northern boundary of Delaware and part of the Mason and Dixon line.

The list of buildings open to visitors is impressive. The Immanuel Church, founded in 1689 and built in 1703, has a set of communion silver, which was a gift from Queen Anne. The Dutch House Museum, believed to be the oldest dwelling in the state, dates from the 17th century. The Amstel House Museum was a splendid residence when it was the site of the wedding reception of Ann Van Dyke, daughter of the then governor. Among the distinguished guests at the reception was George Washington.

OHIO

Guided bus and walking tours are available in German Village, a privately restored section within the city of Columbus. The tours are designed not only to indicate the manner in which urban renewal can be accomplished without federal aid but also to spotlight the Old World architecture of German settlers in the early 1800s.

By 1960 many of the once-splendid structures within the 233-acre historic district had deteriorated. Through the years they had been converted for such uses as rooming houses for transients. Many charming features of the original settlement had vanished—the gardens in miniature courtyards, the arch-type windows, the long, narrow side porches.

The German Village Society was formed to combat the decay and to return the village to its original luster. The City Council gave the society its blessing by creating a German Village Commission and by authorizing publication of a manual covering the architectural control requirements for the area.

Within five years, more than a million dollars in private funds went into the renovation and restoration of more than a hundred homes. What is more important, the distinctive character of the village as a whole began to emerge.

Protected for posterity are the red-brick Dutch residences and the long, lean story-and-a-half houses, built with thick brick walls, cut stone lintels and wrought-iron fences. The restoration embraced a number of stores, many of them three stories tall with proportions and construction details like those of the homes nearby.

Modern materials not in keeping with the early flavor are taboo within the village. The commission's manual states, *Most of the newer types of fences and screens are in most cases obviously out of place. Concrete block screens, wire and cyclone fences are outstanding offenders.*

"Enclosures, in the future, must maintain a rhythm, whether out of brick, iron or wood. Horizontal emphasis directly contradicts the verticality created by the structures and fences now in the

Dock Street Theater along Charleston's History Trail

area. *Wood, although a newer element, can be used successfully."*

The physical restoration brought with it a new pride and a revival of some of the early traditions. The Columbus Männerchor, a German singing society, holds periodic song fests in Schiller Park, just as their forebears did a century ago.

Along with the music and the annual Christmas ritual of lighting a tree in Beck Square, the village sponsors a home and garden tour on the last Sunday in June.

SOUTH CAROLINA

The Trail of History in Charleston, that aristocrat among Southern cities, spans three centuries during which it survived more than its share of war, hurricanes and epidemics. It extends beyond the city into Ansonborough, a suburb where the first permanent colonists in the Carolinas established Charles Towne in 1670, later moving the settlement across the Ashley River to its present peninsula site. It will take you to remnants of the original walled city, dating from the first decades of

Dorr House in Pensacola

the 18th century, and to Fort Sumter, a key fortification during the Civil War.

The trail owes much of its architectural charm to the Historic Foundation of Charleston, created in 1947 to undertake on a grand scale a major restoration and reconstruction of the heart of the old city. The foundation mapped significant buildings within the historic area and imposed controls on demolition, remodeling and new construction. It encouraged individuals and business firms in the area to restore at least the exterior of the buildings they owned. Working with the Preservation Society of Charleston, which had in earlier years rescued a number of old properties, it set up a revolving fund which made possible the purchase of a building, its painstaking restoration, and its sale or rental to those who agreed to maintain the historic property. It bought many of the more than 100 ante-bellum homes in the area and resold them to individuals who expressed a desire to rehabilitate them.

Under this cooperative program, the Preservation Society of Charleston alone has been instrumental in buying and reselling for restoration more than 700 properties, or more than half of those considered worthy of survival. In Ansonborough, the first public high school was remodeled as a private residence, and four classic churches were restored. The revitalization of the area extended to driveways, gardens and courtyards.

GEORGIA

Historic Savannah, perched on a bluff overlooking the Savannah River, retains many historic sites due to the efforts of an organization called Historic Savannah Foundation.

The city offers visitors a map of walking and driving tours, keyed with descriptive information on buildings and parks. It also offers a series of children's tours over bridges and cobblestone streets to riverside museums.

Historic Savannah Foundation began in 1955 with the intent of preserving several buildings and elevated its aim to the revitalization of a two-and-a-half-square-mile area where once-important buildings had degenerated in a slum area. The foundation hired architects and historians to inventory 2500 buildings in the downtown district and learned that 1100 structures were of historic and architectural value. To date, more than half of these have been restored.

The foundation placed the accent on use, discarding the concept of museum preservation. It began with a fund of $200,000 to buy properties and sold buildings at cost to those who agreed to restore them. The success of the program led to the designation of the district by the United States Department of the Interior as a Registered National Historic Landmark.

Visitors come to see not only how near-slum areas have been turned into streets of substance but how fine, old residences have been turned into house museums. These include the Davenport House, headquarters of the foundation and an example of late Georgian architecture. Two other museum houses, both designed by William Jay, are the Owens-Thomas House, visited by Lafayette in 1825, and the birthplace of Juliette Low, founder of the Girl Scouts of America.

MISSOURI

Little-known as a tourist attraction and yet unique in its colonial past is Sainte Geneviève, Missouri, settled by the French in 1735 and the oldest settlement in former Upper Louisiana.

Through architecture and local customs the town retains vestiges of its French heritage, its life under Spanish rule, and its later role as home to German and English settlers. This international mixture is saluted in Jour de Fête à Sainte Geneviève, a community festival held annually the second weekend in August. The name and costumes are French, the participants are of French, German, English and other backgrounds, and the spirit is typically American.

Old landmarks are preserved, restored and maintained by the Foundation for the Historic Restoration of Sainte Geneviève. In addition, a civic organization provides guides and arranges tours of the community.

The walking tour will take you along a number of buildings open to the public. A museum contains such unrelated exhibits as birds mounted by Jean Jacques Audubon and a bank safe allegedly robbed by Jesse James. The Green Tree Tavern was built around the turn of the 18th century by François Janis, a friend of George Rogers Clark, the explorer.

FLORIDA

Pensacola, with its more than 400 years of history, has concentrated its restoration program and its two-hour walking tour around old Seville Square. The restoration, sponsored by the Pensacola Historical Advisory Committee and other city groups, has renewed buildings in more than 25 blocks around the historic square.

French Quarter in New Orleans

121

This was where Creek Indians paraded in 1813 with the damp scalps of 250 persons massacred at nearby Fort Mims. Here, too, General Andrew Jackson's troops battled with the Spanish a year later, and Union soldiers rode their horses over the plot of green during the Civil War.

About the square are such edifices as the Dorr House, restored by the Pensacola Heritage Foundation and used as headquarters by the Historical Advisory Committee. The house, like others nearby, was built in the 1870s when the region was riding high on a lumber boom.

Next door is Old Christ Church (1832), the oldest church in Florida still standing on its original site, and nearby the Dorothy Walton Home (1810) bears the name of an occupant, the widow of a signer of the Declaration of Independence.

LOUISIANA

New Orleans offers the walker or motorist a glimpse into yesteryear in two areas of the city, the Vieux Carré and the Garden District.

The Vieux Carré, the old square or French quarter, founded by the French in 1717, has a harmonious mixture of homes of the Spanish, French, Neo-Classic and Victorian architectural styles. The appearance of the homes and their patios is controlled by a commission which resists modern embellishments.

The Garden District, second oldest residential area of the city, is dotted with mansions, ranging from delicate Georgian to pillared Greek Revival, formerly cloistered on tracts of old plantation sites. Early Americans, many of them planters, built their homes here as showcases of their burgeoning wealth. Some adopted the raised cottage style of upriver plantation homes, while others incorporated stern Eastern seaboard architecture with the softening effect of overhanging iron galleries and shady verandas.

The ideal time to visit the city is during two weeks in the spring when an annual Spring Fiesta is staged. In addition to balls and special cultural events, the fiesta emphasizes tours of homes and gardens in both districts. It also provides tours to historic plantations outside the city.

"Raised cottage" in the Garden District of New Orleans

Ornate balcony of a Vieux Carré home in New Orleans

ARKANSAS

Washington, Arkansas, describes its walking tour as a look into the past. The community is the oldest incorporated town in the state, the place where the Texas revolution against Mexico was plotted and the home of the Bowie knife.

In its early days, the town was strategically important because of its location along the Chihuahua Trail, a route which took thousands of settlers into the West. A tavern, Traveler's Inn, was built in 1830 to accommodate the increasing number of pioneers. Its tap room became a gathering place for such frontiersmen as Davy Crockett, Colonel James Bowie and Sam Houston. Today, the tavern is the headquarters of Pioneer Washington, an organization which provides guides for tourists. The guides will lead you to such spots as the Confederate State Capitol, now a museum and a memorial; the James Black blacksmith shop, where the original Bowie knife was fashioned; and a number of pioneer homes open to the public.

NEBRASKA

Like many other communities, Brownville, a "village of memories" on the Missouri River, provides a walking tour throughout the year and special events during summer months. The events

Birthplace of the Bowie knife

vary from a tour of homes to a fine arts' day and an old fiddlers' contest.

Brownville, founded in 1854, was a frontier town of the Missouri River steamboat days. It was a "cow town" in the 1860s, when longhorns from the cattle trails were ferried across the river. It was also a jumping-off and restocking place for settlers headed West. Brownville prospered and grew until the railroad bypassed it, prompting officials to place the county seat at Auburn. Streets which once bustled with cattlemen, pioneers and boat crews became comparatively silent.

Realizing its tourist potential, the Brownville Historical Society has restored a number of structures and placed markers at historical sites. Walking along Main Street from the river front, the tourist may inspect the old Lone Tree Saloon, reputedly visited many times by Jesse James, and the site of the land office where Daniel Freeman signed for the first official homestead in the nation. The visitor may also take in brick houses of the riverboat era and a number of churches and museums.

WISCONSIN

Mineral Point, settled in 1827, was a boisterous, booming lead mining camp which attracted Cornish miners, or Cousin Jacks, as they were called. Talented as stone masons, they built so well that many of the old buildings constructed in the Old World tradition still stand.

A walking tour of historic sites in Mineral Point cuts across an irregular pattern of streets, many of them determined by the paths of early miners, to Shake Rag Street with its restored Cornish homes. Pendarvis is the general name for the complex of Cornish rock and log houses built in the 1830s and restored a century later by Robert M. Neal and Edgar Hellum, two men whose concern for antiquity halted the deterioration of the historic area. The houses are solidly built, the fronts of dressed stone and the side and rear walls of uncut stone.

A tour will guide you to early churches and the homes of such pioneers as Moses M. Strong, a U.S. district attorney and in 1846 delegate to the first Constitutional Convention.

CALIFORNIA

In California, Monterey and San Diego are among the cities which have mapped historic walking tours.

Monterey, once the Spanish heart of California, became a part of the Mexican Republic in 1822 and an American territory 24 years later. Its Path of History is marked by an orange-red line painted down the center of streets, leading to houses of distinction. The most significant points along the path are 11 sites and structures maintained by the state as historic monuments. Marked by a monument is Serra Landing Site where Sebastian Vizcaino landed in 1602 and where, on June 3, 1770, Fray Junípero Serra and Don Gaspar de Portola held religious services, giving thanks for a safe journey and founding Monterey. A two-story home, known as Stevenson House, put up Robert Louis Stevenson as a boarder in the autumn of 1879.

At the Custom House, with its tile roof extending over wide porches, the United States flag was officially raised by Commodore John Drake Sloat in 1846. Nearby is California's first theater, begun as a lodging house and barroom. Today, 19th century plays are presented weekly by the Troupers of the Golden Coast, making the building a living monument.

San Diego, where the Portuguese conquistador Cabrillo landed in 1540, places its walking tour emphasis on "Old Town, where California began." A green line here will lead you to points of greatest interest. The city has developed a 230-acre region as a historic area. In 16 acres set apart as a Registered National Historic Landmark is the Presidio, which holds the same significance for California as do Jamestown and Plymouth for the Atlantic seaboard. It commemorates the founding of the first permanent European settlement on the Pacific Coast and the establishment of the first mission, San Diego de Alcalá, by Junípero Serra.

In other areas the city has been restoring ancient buildings, turning a number of them into museums. It has also been placing utility lines underground and replacing cement pavements with footpaths.

In the historic area is a heady mixture of old Spanish and early American. The Casa de Lopez (1835) is a restored adobe dwelling, while the Pendleton House (1851) is an early prefabricated house of Maine lumber, shipped around the Horn and assembled with pegs. The Whaley House (1857) was built of hand-made bricks by merchant Thomas Whaley, and the adobe home built by John Brown (1850) later served as San Diego's first church outside Presidio walls. Artifacts in the Junípero Serra Historical Museum in Presidio Park trace the history of California and the missions for which it is famous.

Brownville, Nebraska, a "village of memories"

125

12 *A Directory of Museum Villages*

FOLLOWING IS A LISTING, by states, of museum villages in the United States.

ALASKA

Alaskaland, near Fairbanks, a relocated gold rush log cabin town created from 19th and early 20th century buildings. The 40-acre site includes a Native Village where Eskimos, Indians and Aleut natives demonstrate their crafts. Open daily Memorial Day through Labor Day. Admission.

Port Chilkoot-Haines, site of Totem Village, built by the Chilkat Indian Dancers. The village, created around an Indian Tribal House, includes replicas of Indian and trapper structures. Open all year. Admission.

ARIZONA

Canyon de Chelly National Monument, ruins of several hundred prehistoric Indian villages. Admission.

Navajo National Monument, ruins of prehistoric cliff dwelling villages. Admission.

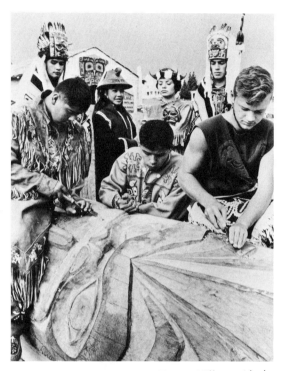

Totem Village, Alaska

Casa Grande National Monument, near Coolidge, Indian ruins built some 600 years ago by the Hohokam as a fort, watchtower and apartment house. Open all year. Admission.

Tombstone, a former silver mining and Wild West town which has restored many early structures. Admission charge to buildings which are now museums.

Old Tucson, a fun-type replica of a Wild West town, built and still being used as a movie set. Open all year. Admission.

Tuzigoot National Monument, remnants of prehistoric town built by Indians. Admission.

ARKANSAS

Bull Shoals, recreated mountain village of 1890. Open all year. Admission.

Old Tavern, Washington, Arkansas

Little Rock, the *Arkansas Territorial Capital Restoration,* occupies most of a city block and provides a picture of life in the 1820s. Open all year. Admission.

Prairie Grove, replica of pioneer village in Prairie Grove Battlefield Park.

Washington, which calls itself "The Cradle of Arkansas History," has reconstructed and restored buildings to preserve an antebellum atmosphere. Open all year. Admission for each open home or museum.

CALIFORNIA

Bakersfield, extensive pioneer village on a 12-acre site with buildings tracing the history of Kern County. Open all year. Admission.

Barstow, nearby *Calico Ghost Town* is an old silver mining and ghost town that was privately restored and deeded to the county of San Bernardino. Open all year.

Bodie State Historic Park, gold-mining ghost town, once known throughout the West for its wickedness, is maintained in a state of "arrested decay."

Buena Park, *Knott's Berry Farm and Ghost Town* combine a restaurant operation with a re-created town of gold rush days. Open all year. Free admission, but fees for individual attractions.

Columbia State Historic Park, gold rush town preserved by the state to recall a colorful era in American history.

Fort Ross State Historic Park, restoration of a tiny hamlet that was once the outpost of the Russian empire. Open all year. Free.

Monterey, "Path of History" leads to every old house of distinction. A walking tour.

San Diego, a walking tour places the emphasis on "Old Town, where California began." Early Spanish and American homes have been restored and are open to the public.

COLORADO

Buckskin Joe, restored mining town of the 1860–70s, "romanticized" for the entertainment of visitors with re-enactment of shoot-outs. Open summer months. Admission.

Manitou Springs, *Manitou Cliff Dwellings Museum,* a collection of cliff dwellings dating from 1000 to 1300 A.D. Open all year. Admission.

Mesa Verde National Park, cliff city ruins which tell the story of 2000 years of Indian life before the arrival of the white man.

Russia once occupied Fort Ross, California

CONNECTICUT

Mystic Seaport, the re-creation of a 19th century New England coastal village through 40 buildings on 37 acres. Open all year. Admission.

FLORIDA

Pensacola, a walking tour of historic sites and restored homes that have played a part in the city's past. Some homes and museums along the way are open to the public.

St. Augustine, the re-creation and restoration of a complex of buildings, built during the years of Spanish rule. Open all year. Admission charge for each historic structure.

Tallahassee, *Junior Museum* on Lake Bradford includes a pioneer farm restoration on 40 acres. Open all year. Free.

GEORGIA

New Echota, state-owned re-creation of village which served as the Eastern Cherokee capital from 1825 to 1838. Open all year. Admission.

Savannah, a walking tour of *Old Savannah,* America's first planned city. Much of the early center has been restored with private funds.

Stone Mountain Memorial Park, a restored 18-building complex, furnished in period, representing a plantation village. Open all year.

HAWAII

Laie, the Polynesian Cultural Center with six villages depicting the lives and culture of six South Seas tribes. Villages, which have craft demonstrations, native songs and dances, reflect early life in Samoa, Maori, Fiji, Tahiti, Hawaii and Tonga. Open all year. Admission.

ILLINOIS

Bishop Hill, the living restoration of the first major Swedish settlement in the Midwest. The town was founded by the Janssonists, religious dissenters, in the mid-19th century.

Nauvoo, restoration of a town that was a Mormon center briefly and went into limbo after the Mormons headed for the Great Salt Lake in Utah in 1847.

New Salem State Park, recreation of the town in which Abraham Lincoln lived from 1831 to 1837. Open all year. Free.

INDIANA

Hamilton, the *Conner Prairie Settlement* reflects life of the early pioneers and fur traders.

New Harmony, restored town founded by the Rappites as an experiment in communal living and later (1825) taken over by Robert Owen, Scottish industrialist, for his great social experiment.

Polynesian life at Laie, Hawaii

Lincoln Village, Indiana

Rockport, *Lincoln Pioneer Village,* a memorial with period buildings and furnishings to Abraham Lincoln and his 14 years in Spencer County. Open all year. Admission.

IOWA

Amana Colonies, a historic living village, settled by a German religious sect in the mid-1800s as a community dedicated to the principles of communal life. The seven villages of the Amanas later adopted the free enterprise system and survive today as prosperous communities.

Bentonsport, a once-prosperous steamboat-era town which has preserved many early buildings.

West Branch, *Herbert Hoover Birthplace.* The President's birthplace, library, museum and gravesite are set off by adjacent streets which have been restored to their appearance at the time of Hoover's birth. Open all year.

Hoover Birthplace

KANSAS

Old Abilene, a replica of Abilene during the cattle boom, includes some original buildings of the era.

Dodge City, Historic Front Street is a reproduction of a block where the action took place in the days of the Wild West.

Wichita has *Cowtown,* a 35-building museum village, showing how things were in the era of the cattle drives. Closed in winter. Admission.

KENTUCKY

Shakertown at Pleasant Hill, the restoration of a major Shaker village located high above the

Loreauville, Louisiana

palisades of the Kentucky River. Open all year. Admission.

Springfield, the *Lincoln Homestead State Shrine* is a compound of restored and reconstructed buildings related to the lives of Abraham Lincoln's parents and grandparents. Open summer months. Admission.

LOUISIANA

Loreauville, *Loreauville Heritage Museum,* the re-creation of an authentic Acadian village. Open all year. Admission.

New Orleans, walking tour of the French quarter. Homes and gardens open during two weeks in the spring.

129

MASSACHUSETTS

Deerfield, a "living village" restoration with more than 30 buildings at least 150 years old. A few buildings open all year, others during summer months. Admission to individual buildings.

Hancock, *Hancock Shaker Village,* an outstanding restoration of a long-lived Shaker center. Open summer months. Admission.

Plymouth, *Plimoth Plantation,* the re-creation of the Pilgrim village as it was a few years after they landed. Planned are an Indian village and a later Pilgrim community. Open summer months. Admission.

Salem, *Pioneer Village,* reproduction of Salem as it was in 1630. Open summer months. Admission.

Shop at Dearborn

MINNESOTA

Brainerd, *Lumbertown USA,* replica of a typical old-time lumber town with full-size operating replica of first Northern Pacific train. Open summer months. Admission.

Fort Mille Lacs, re-created Indian village on the Chippewa (Ojibway) Indian Reservation. Indian craft demonstrations, tribal dances. Open summer months. Free.

MISSISSIPPI

Natchez, walking tour along streets "where the Old South still lives." Antebellum homes, gardens and plantations open during "Natchez Pilgrimage" in March.

At Old Sturbridge Village

Sturbridge, *Old Sturbridge Village,* re-creation of a New England community reflecting rural life from 1790 to 1840. Site includes an early farm complex. Planned is the re-creation of a manufacturing village. Open all year. Admission.

West Springfield, *Storrowton,* village of 12 buildings represents a New England village from late 18th to early 19th century. Open summer months. Free.

MICHIGAN

Dearborn, *Henry Ford Museum* and *Greenfield Village,* one of the country's greatest museums combined with a village of nearly 100 historic buildings. Open all year. Admission.

Lumbertown in Minnesota

MISSOURI

Sainte Geneviève, walking tour through town which retains its French heritage. Nine structures, including homes and museums, open to the public, some free.

Silver Dollar City, the Ozarks' 1880 frontier village with craft demonstrations, seasonal "Root Digging Days" and "National Festival of Craftsmen." Closed in winter. Admission.

Village of St. François, *Yesterday USA,* recreated Ozark pioneer village of 1734 to 1890 with 30 buildings on 700 acres. Open all year. Admission.

MONTANA

Frontier Town, located near Helena, replica of early Western town built of native stone and logs. Typical buildings, including chapel, jail and

Silver Dollar, Missouri

Stanton Hall, Natchez

shops, were built and authentically furnished by one man, John R. Quigley, as a tribute to frontier forebears. Open summer months.

Nevada City and *Virginia City,* two former gold mining towns in Alder Gulch. Nevada City, a ghost town by the end of the 19th century, has had its main buildings restored and furnished as museums. Virginia City is a "living museum village" which has tried to recapture the feeling of the gold rush days.

NEBRASKA

Brownville, a "village of memories" on the Missouri River, has mapped a walking tour along historic streets. Some structures, including homes and museums, open to the public.

Grand Island, *Stuhr Museum* on island in man-made lake houses prairie pioneer exhibits. Outdoor museum has turn-of-century village, country church, log cabins, Indian village, demonstration areas. Open all year. Admission.

Minden, *Harold Warp Pioneer Village,* 22 buildings on 20 acres re-creating man's technological progress since 1830. Open all year. Admission.

NEW HAMPSHIRE

Canterbury, restoration in progress of a major Shaker village. A few sisters continue to reside in a brick residence. A Shaker museum is housed in the original Meetinghouse.

Portsmouth, Strawbery Banke, an outstanding restoration of structures which mirror the progress of this seaport community. Open summer months. Admission.

Virginia City stagecoach

131

NEW JERSEY

Allaire State Park, a once-prosperous iron making village, later a ghost town, has been restored much as it was in the 1850s. Closed winter months. Admission.

Batsto, *Batsto State Historic Site,* restored village which flourished in the days when bog ore was important for the production of iron. Open all year. Admission.

Smithville, partial restoration of late 18th century community, including inn, general store, grist mill and a score of other buildings. Open all year.

Waterloo Village, a dozen homes and outbuildings restored and furnished, some dating back to 1760. Open all year. Admission.

NEW MEXICO

Aztec Ruins National Monument, near Farmington, ruins of one of the largest pre-Spanish villages in the Southwest. Open all year. Admission.

Chaco Canyon National Monument, Indian ruins include those of an apartment house, built from 800 to 1100 A.D. for more than 1000 persons. Open all year. Admission.

Gila Cliff Dwellers National Monument, trails to cliff dwellings about 180 feet above the canyon floor. Open all year. Admission.

NEW YORK

Auburn, *Owasco Stockaded Indian Village,* reconstruction reflecting the height of Owasco culture about 1150 A.D. Open summer months. Admission.

Cooperstown, *Farmers' Museum* and its *Village Crossroads,* a re-creation of life in rural New York between 1783 and the 1840s. Open all year. Admission.

Monroe, *Museum Village of Smith's Clove,* re-created village demonstrating how American industry evolved from the days of homespun to giant industry. Open warm-weather months. Admission.

New Paltz, stone houses built by the Huguenots in the 17th and 18th centuries along "the oldest street in America with its original houses." House museum open all year, others during summer months. Donation.

Richmondtown, re-creation on Staten Island of a typical American village of the 18th and 19th century in the center of Metropolitan New York. Some buildings open all year. Admission.

Geauga County, Ohio

NORTH CAROLINA

Cherokee, *Oconaluftee Indian Village,* replica of Indian village of two centuries ago on Qualla Reservation. Open summer months. Admission.

Winston-Salem, *Old Salem,* former planned community established by the Moravians. Many structures restored and furnished, with early crafts demonstrated in shops. Exhibit buildings open all year. Admission.

NORTH DAKOTA

Medora, village restored to the days when Theodore Roosevelt ranched in the area. The Rough Rider Hotel takes in guests, and visitors can see ranching and rodeo skills demonstrated through the summer.

Old Salem, North Carolina

Western Reserve, Ohio

OHIO

Bath, *Pioneer Farm Museum* and *Western Reserve Village,* administered by the Western Reserve Historical Society. Village represents life in the Western Reserve up to 1850. Open summer months.

Burton, *Geauga County Museum and Village,* buildings moved to area to create typical village of the 1850–60s. Seasonal events. Open all year. Admission.

Canfield, *Pioneer Village in Canfield Fairgrounds,* typical early Western Reserve Village. Grounds open all year, tours by appointment. Free.

Columbus, *German Village,* walking tour of restored structures with Old World architectural details with some buildings open to the public. Seasonal public events.

Defiance, *Au Glaize Village,* collection of restored buildings, many moved from other areas, depicting village in 1860–90 period. Open all year with a variety of special events from April through November.

Morgan Township, *Governor Bebb Park* and *Log Village,* partially furnished log structures representative of an early 19th century village, administered by the Butler County Park District.

New Philadelphia, reproduction of first Moravian Mission settlement in Ohio, 1772, with cabins, school and church. Open all year. Free.

Zoar, state-owned heart of a communal village established by Zoarites in the early 19th century and dissolved in 1898. A number of restored homes and gardens are open to the public during warm-weather months.

OKLAHOMA

Anadarko, *Indian City,* authentic reconstruction of villages of several Plains tribes, with Indian guides. Open all year. Admission.

Talequah, *Tsa-la-gi,* a re-creation of an Indian village prior to the white man's arrival, with guides and craft demonstrations. Open all year.

OREGON

Florence, *Indian Forest,* full-size replicas of assorted Indian dwellings set along a trail in a 20-acre wilderness.

PENNSYLVANIA

Ambridge, *Old Economy Village,* one of three villages established by the Harmony Society in the 19th century, restored and filled with relics. Open summer months. Admission.

Avella, *Meadowcraft Village,* 32 structures moved to re-create a farming community. Open all year. Admission.

Bethlehem, portion of an 18th century Moravian settlement, with a number of buildings and museums open to the public.

Cornwall, 18th century ironworks and nearby miners' village. Furnace maintained by the Pennsylvania Historical Commission. Open all year. Admission.

Ephrata, *Ephrata Cloister,* celibate community established in 1732 by German Pietists. The monastic community, which numbered 300 followers, has been restored and furnished. Open all year. Admission.

Hopewell Village National Historic Site, village built around charcoal-burning iron furnace restored to 1820–40 period. Open all year.

Lancaster, *Pennsylvania Farm Museum of Landis Valley,* state-supervised farm museum with period homes, craft shops, and more than 250,000 items. Open all year. Admission.

Indian City, Oklahoma

133

SOUTH CAROLINA

Charleston, walking tour of Trail of History spanning three centuries. Many historic buildings preserved by the Preservation Society of Charleston.

Spartanburg, *Walnut Grove Plantation*, re-creation of an antebellum plantation community. Open all year. Admission.

SOUTH DAKOTA

Prairie Village, near Madison, a reproduction of an 1890 prairie village, with annual threshing jamborees in August. Open summer months. Admission.

Alamo Village, Texas

Walnut Grove, South Carolina

TENNESSEE

Gatlinburg, *Homespun Valley Mountaineer Village*, working replica of village of early mountaineer days. Open summers. Admission.

Memphis, *Chucalissa Indian Village and Museum*, Indian village founded about 900 and abandoned in 1600s, excavated and preserved by the Memphis State University. Open all year.

Nashville, *Old Hickory's Hermitage*, complex including two mansions associated with Andrew Jackson and a number of outbuildings. Maintained by the Ladies Hermitage Association. Open all year. Admission.

TEXAS

Alamo Village, near San Antonio, reproduction of an Old West Texas town, built in 1959 as a movie set and now operated as a tourist attraction. Open all year. Admission.

Corsicana, *Pioneer Village in Beauford Jester Park*, with restored log structures, including blacksmith shop and grist mill. Open summer

months through week, winter Sundays only. Donation.

Fort Worth, *Log Cabin Village in Forest Park*, municipally owned group of pioneer homes used by early settlers. Open all year. Admission.

Livingston, *Living Indian Village*, located on Texas' only Indian Reservation, home of the Alabama and Coushatta tribes. Village re-creating an 1805 setting has craft demonstrations. Open all year. Admission.

Wimberley, *Pioneertown*, re-creation of a town of the Old West, circa 1880, as part of a resort area. Open summer months.

VERMONT

Shelburne, *Shelburne Museum*, mammoth and tasteful outdoor museum of early American buildings with furnishings and exhibits covering a wide range of Americana. Open summer months. Admission.

Fort Worth, Texas

Shelburne, Vermont

VIRGINIA

Appomattox Court House National Historic Park, small but historic community where General Lee officially surrendered his Confederate forces to General Grant. Open all year.

Hampton, *Kicotan Indian Village,* replica of dwellings of Indians who lived in Virginia when the English landed in Hampton.

Jamestown Festival Park, state-owned re-creation of the original settlement, including full-scale sailing models of the three ships, *Susan Constant, Godspeed* and *Discovery.* Open all year. Admission.

Williamsburg, *Colonial Williamsburg,* painstaking restoration of the 18th-century capital of Virginia, undertaken at a cost of more than $76 million by John D. Rockefeller Jr. Open all year. Admission.

WASHINGTON

Cashmere, *Willis Carey Museum,* original buildings and replica of old mission represent a pioneer village. Open summer months.

WEST VIRGINIA

Harpers Ferry National Historic Park, reconstruction of a once-prosperous town devastated by the Civil War. This was the site of John Brown's ill-fated attempt to seize federal arms.

WISCONSIN

Paul Bunyan Camp, re-created logging camp with 19th century tools and furnishings. Open summer months. Free.

Mineral Point, walking tour of restored homes of Cornish lead miners. Guided tours for groups for a charge.

Stonefield, a composite of small Midwestern villages of the last century, with replicas of shops lining a village green. Open summer months. Admission.

WYOMING

Fort Laramie National Historic Site, re-created Army post along the Oregon Trail, once a fortified village. Open all year.

South Pass City, gold rush town restored by state long after it became a ghost town. Open summer months.

Pioneer Village at the Willis Carey Museum, Washington

Photo Credits

Frontispiece, New Jersey Department of Conservation and Economic Development; 6 Colonial Williamsburg; 8 New Mexico Department of Development; 9 Idaho Department of Commerce and Development; 10 Strawbery Banke; 11 Hale Farm Museum; 12, 13 Stewarts; 14 Illinois Division of Parks; 16 Arizona State Department of Economic Planning and Development; 18, 19 U.S. National Park Service; 20 New Mexico Department of Development; 21 Tennessee Division of Information and Tourist Promotion; 22 North Carolina Department of Conservation and Development; 23 Cherokee Historical Association; 24 Microfilm Division, Georgia Department of State; 25 Indian City; 26 Hampton Information Bureau; 27 Finger Lakes Association; 28, 30, 31 Jamestown Foundation; 32 Plimoth Plantation; 33 Pioneer Village; 35 Colonial Williamsburg; 36 Virginia Department of Conservation and Economic Development; 37, 38 Strawbery Banke; 39–41 Florida Development Commission; 42–45 Shelburne Museum; 46, 47 Old Sturbridge Village; 48 Connecticut Development Commission; 51 Stone Mountain Park; 53 B & B Studio; 54 Louisiana Tourist Development Commission; 55–57 Henry Ford Museum; 59 Jonathan Hale Homestead; 60 Ohio Department of Development; 61 Ohio Historical Society; 62 Arkansas Territorial Restoration; 63 Arkansas Publicity and Parks Commission; 64 Indiana State Department of Commerce; 66, 67 Nebraska State Game Commission; 68 Pioneer Village; 70 Colorado Department of Public Relations; 71–74 California State Office of Tourism; 75–77 Montana Highway Commission; 78, 79 Wyoming Travel Commission; 81 West Virginia Department of Commerce; 82 Virginia Department of Conservation and Economic Development; 84 Lincoln Heritage Trail; 85 Indiana Department of Commerce; 86 Illinois Division of Tourism; 87 Lincoln Heritage Trail; 89, 90 North Dakota Travel Division; 91 Old Tucson; 92 Kansas Department of Economic Development; 93 Wyoming Travel Commission; 94–97 Pennsylvania Historical and Museum Commission; 98 Michael Manheim; 99, 100 Iowa Development Commission; 102, 103 Shakertown; 104, 105 Old Salem; 106 Illinois Department of Business and Economic Development; 107 Illinois Division of Parks; 108 Batsto; 111, 112 Lebanon Valley Tourist Bureau; 113 U. S. National Park Service; 115 Lumbertown; 116, 117 Delaware State Development Department; 119 State of South Carolina; 120 Florida Development Commission; 121–123 New Orleans Festival Association; 124 Arkansas Publicity and Parks Commission; 125 Nebraska Game Commission; 126 (bottom) Arkansas Publicity and Parks Commission, (top) Alaska Travel Division; 127 California Division of Beaches and Parks; 128 Polynesia Cultural Center; 129 (top left) Indiana Department of Commerce, (bottom left) Iowa Department of Commerce, (right) Louisiana Tourist Development Commission; 130 (left) Old Sturbridge Village, (top right) Henry Ford Museum, (bottom right) Minnesota Division of Publicity; 131 (left) Mississippi Agricultural and Industrial Board, (top right) Silver Dollar City, (bottom right) Far West Studio; 132 (left) North Carolina Department of Conservation and Development, (right) Ohio Development Commission; 133 (top) Ohio Development Commission, (bottom) American Petroleum Institute; 134 (left) Spartanburg City Historical Association, (top right) Alamo Village, (bottom right) City of Fort Worth; 135 (top) Shelburne Museum, (bottom) Washington Department of Commerce and Economic Development.

DATE DUE

MY F7 '80			
GAYLORD			PRINTED IN U.S.A.